What To Do

When The Wheels Come Off

Strange observations and reckless advice about life and disability

Michael J. Giusti

DEDICATION

This book is especially dedicated to my sister Mrs. Mary Fenton and to all those wonderful people throughout my life that have helped me transcend my disabilities.

They specifically include Mr. Cameron M. Arnoult, Mr. Luke Garris, Mrs. Karen Gifford, Dr. Aron Culotta, and Mr. Joshua Peter Morant.

Michael J Giusti

CONTENTS

ACKNOWLEDGMENTS

I would like to acknowledge the following kind people who were the first to encourage me to write. They include Mrs. Marie Louise Nix, Mrs. Pamela Binnings Ewen, Mr. Andy Antippas, and Mr. Elton Lala. I would also like to express my appreciation to Dr. Aron Culotta for his high intelligence and superior patience throughout the tedious editing process.

Lastly, I would like to specially recognize Mr. Cameron Arnoult for his unfailing support and Mr. Luke Garris for allowing me to use both his photographic talent and treasure to illustrate the book.

In addition to the author's portrait, other works by Mr. Garris appear on pages 10, 41, 57, 114, 144, and 154. The images on page 5 and 60 are credited to Mr. Ryan Mc Guire from Gratisography and a nice photograph by Mr. Russell Burden appears on page 71. Finally a photo attributed to the National Museum of American History appears on page 128.

If I had been better organized and had listened to my friends more carefully, I would have had this work published long ago.

Preface

"The feeling remains God is on the journey too."

The words that follow are not as profound as those of Saint Teresa of Avila but they inspired the creation of this practical little book.

We operate well only when we learn to overcome the wreckage we create and try to fix the damage we see. Inside is a new look at some very old concepts. But first, it may be a good idea for me to heed Mr. Kipling's warning: "Don't look too good, nor talk too wise."

I am just a regular guy from New Orleans and with daily use of a wheelchair I thought I had an unusual and healthy perspective on life. I never really allowed anything to stop me; then Katrina happened. This is not just another storm account or an inspirational story about a handicapped dude. It's an introspective search from a man trying to find traction again after the wheels came off his life. My journey takes the form of short humorous proverbs, blended with some rather provocative ideas. It is easy to read and designed so that anyone can pick it up and get a boost.

I wrote this book because I believe that we all need to think more kindly and step more carefully through the imposing world we navigate. An impossible journey can become much less laborious once we learn to give more attention and respect to our blessings, talents, and responsibilities. Friends and family know that we can read and see, but only we can reflect on the obstacles God has given us and share in the precision they have taught us.

Some ideas may come across as preachy, self-righteous, or full of bravado. Sadly my progress remains incomplete. But I hope you may still want to go on this ride with me and join in the fun and excitement of what to do........ "When the Wheels Come Off."

1

JOURNEY BEGINS

5 Year Old Kids

What if my goal today is to make you smile, laugh and feel more secure? Let's play like we are 5 years old again!

Attitude

Acceptance

We all begin our journey as innocent creatures just trying to find our way through many unexpected turns and steep learning curves. One of the first hard lessons I had to learn was not to allow anyone the power to impose their negative standards on me in order to gain their approval. As a handicapped kid, all I ever wanted was acceptance and I quickly learned that the best way to receive affirmation was through a healthy attitude.

Our gifts often resemble our needs. We all want friends who like us, as we are, untouched, less refined and unfinished. And as we mature we must find our support free from the expectations and desires of anyone. Judgment always has a way of coming back on us. We all come from each other and are all of the same flesh. We are not similar to God in His love. We are exactly the same. He alone knows the evidence of our life and only He may hold the gavel and key.

The kindest hearts already know that acceptance does not mean consent, but it often inspires a transcendent love that encourages growth. Our humanity is best demonstrated through our shared experience. So our safest choice is one of life's oldest instructions:

"Let us do unto others as we would have them do unto us."

Behavior

Accountant

It's always better to be our brother's accountant rather than his keeper. Then we can hire someone else to clean his cage.

Behavior

Actual Help

An ounce of actual help is worth a pound of preaching.

Authenticity

Aid

Something as simple as a helping hand can be offered on every occasion. The great gift, of course, is in the kind gesture itself, but I must share with you a well-hidden secret from the handicapped code book. Most of us actually do need some kind of aid, but a few are a little proud to ask for help. Please save us from our hubris and always extend a strong hand anyway.

The aging of my booming generation has increased our ranks dramatically. So every kindness is noted and appreciated.

Help

Always

Of all the admonitions we should try to use to help us, no thought is more useful than this: "Smart wins." This creative intelligence is always available when we have the courage to want it, but we must also be wise enough to recognize the people who have it.

Search for the Solomons in your life. They are easy to spot because they never divide people and seem to like children.

Wisdom

Anthem

Our deepest truth is best enjoyed through personal action, but it is not always convenient for us. This is because warm thoughts, kind words, and good intentions are very easy to produce, and they provide an excellent cover for our continued laziness. It's the very reason why most "To Do" lists wither into "Never Done" lists.

Although action is often difficult, it can help in any direction when we realize we are surrounded by unmet need. All of us have been created to live as an action hero. Sadly some of us would rather mark time and collect dust in the hope of being rescued by one.

Action

Artifact

It's true we are all unique creations, but we are also templates of our ancestors. The best way to honor their memory is to become the model for our children that our parents were for us...........

Memory

Assessment

The smartest thing we can do is shift our attention away from those who wish to remain ignorant and focus more on those who want to grow. This is especially important for our own internal assessment.

Awareness

Associate

Associate with people who are interested in making you laugh and run from those who try to make you feel guilty. A giggle is more helpful than a deep thought and a smile is much better than the fulfillment of a deep obligation.

Relationships

Biggest

Be wary around the largest personality or the loudest voice. They didn't spend much time in study hall.

Authenticity

Bright Idea

No one can ever become a light for us until we provide a good connection to them.

Guidance

Brightest People

The best way to comfort a buddy is to lighten our own load first. It is impossible to help another person when we are in need of a sky cap ourselves. We should discard our old baggage sometimes even when it is attractive simply because it may be too expensive to carry for the long haul. When we become lighter, we can more easily be a guiding light for someone else. The brightest people are never hard to spot because they always know how to help everybody lighten up!

Guidance

Buzz

Wise people learn all about the bee without experience of the stinger.

Relationships

Calm

Over-reactions often disrupt good opportunities. It would have been an even cooler story if all 13 guys could have just relaxed and walked on the water during the storm.

Behavior

Captivate

Have you noticed that many of the pundits and social commentators seem to lack consideration, gravitas, solemnity or even an advanced education? Does every serious discussion have to be led by a second rate comedian from a fake dining room set?

Give me a thoughtful exchange from people of advanced experience who understand the power of language. Then allow them the chance to defend their opinion with intelligence, wisdom, and wit. It can do more than just entertain us. It can captivate us in such a way that we may want to join in the discussion and try to solve some problems.

Solutions

Caution

Doubt is not always a bad thing because we are sometimes misguided by our gullibility and false assumptions. Often what we think of as doubt is just some native wisdom trying to warn us that the road ahead may not be as wide as we think or as smooth as we want.

Guidance

Chip In

We have all heard the old expression that we cannot help everyone. But if our interest is music, writing, farming, education, spiritual development, crime prevention, health care, or many other pursuits, every person that we can reach may benefit in some way.

Whenever we address a problem or refuse to become part of an obstruction, we have just helped make everything better. Anytime we use any talent as an unselfish resource, we have contributed to every part of humanity. Each one of us was formed to enrich the world. We can and do help everyone if only through our prayers and creative attitude. All that is necessary is our willingness to chip in!

Generosity

15

Closely Separate

Look closely into a child's eyes to see every person created.
In heart, mind, body, and soul we are all separately related.

Brotherly Love

Company

Whenever someone tries to manipulate your experience with God,
gently understand the loneliness of their misery and invite them to
seek the quiet company of their architect.

Manipulation

Concocted

The older I get the more I admire a person who is willing to share his
doubts. Self-assurance is a good thing, but so often it seems
concocted for public consumption. I could be wrong about this, but
I doubt it.

Faith

Coolest Thing

The coolest thing about confidence is that when we choose to
possess it, it also helps everyone around us. Confidence is like every
gift we are given. It only becomes a gift the moment we give it away.

Confidence

Could Be

Who we are is always a little less than who we could be. We were created as vital, dynamic creatures able to grow, learn, choose, and change. Better choices arrive every day hoping to be selected.

Growth

Crosswalk

Whenever we find ourselves in a difficult space,
let's change our minds to a more peaceful place.

It never really matters what happens to us,
because we are not there to be hit by a bus.

Attitude

Curtain

What is the impulse that allows us to change the channel when we see a starving child or quicken our pace past a homeless man? It is not really hatred; it's just a faint antipathy that causes such a distance. It is deep, dark, subtle and smooth. It is the simple loss of empathy for creatures that no longer look like us.

A friend once told me of his visit to Poland shortly after the Iron Curtain fell. It wasn't the extreme poverty that shocked him so much. It was the fact that he had never seen so many "white people" suffering in the ghetto at one time.

Empathy

Cut It

For me, words don't seem to cut it as well anymore. I don't know if talk is cheaper now, but it sure seems a lot more plentiful. Because I am a person in a wheelchair, I often cannot get to all the things I need. My first hope is always that someone will come along and reach for me rather than preach to me.

Actions

Deep Breath

The difference between a life well lived and anything less comes from our ability to share inspiration. Encouraging molecules wash around us every moment unless we choose to live a more vacuous life. Sometimes they give us the courage to step into the ring and sometimes they challenge us to know when to step out again. But either way, our best hope always includes the clarity and good choices our inspirations can provide.

Sometimes good friends choose an easy and early exit for lack of this encouragement. But before they are forced horizontal by a sad and breathless choice, we must try to give to them a measure of our own vitality. From our wisp of faith, new hope can sometimes emerge. A true hero knows how to pump life into his friend so that he may also become heroic again. There is no magic in the effort. We just need to be willing to share the celestial breath given to us. It can bring life to everything because it is life itself.

Inspiration

Cue

Unhappiness is just God's cue to encourage us to love, and His Son often allows us to cut first in line.

Opportunity

Deserve

A creative way to reduce our need is to simply become more grateful. Gratitude is an amazing creature. He expands our treasure, gives us keener eyesight, and also makes room for more blessings. The moment we become friends with gratitude we realize that we both deserve him and possess him.

Gratitude

Difference

The moment we invite people to think differently, we have already begun to make a difference.

Attitude

Dig

Just under the rubble of the things we destroy, our tenacity waits patiently for its next great opportunity. It often hides from us, especially when it feels ignored. But it still remains the foundation for our character and the cornerstone of our faith. Ever present, beneath the surface, true resolve can move us away from our poor choices and allow us to become a measure for our better attributes. So whenever we cannot see or feel our personal courage at work, all we need to do is get busy and dig!

Tenacity

Direction

When the wind knocks out of your sails, don't worry! It's just nature's way of changing direction.

Guidance

Double Trouble

People who live a double life add twice as much trouble to our own.

Authenticity

Duck

As a small child with a disability, I was taught never to be too concerned with why the chicken crossed the road but rather to focus on finding out how he did it. This small adjustment in my thinking has really helped me throughout my life.

Whenever I closely analyzed any situation that I could not change, I realized "why" only had the power to sap my strength.

I have always been a little roundabout(??) in my problem solving. In addition to working hard to help other chickens get to the other side, it took me years to figure out how to get "down" from an elephant because I never could understand how I got up there in the first place!

Attitude

Easy

Fear has a greater ability to take hold of us when we are not involved in a better activity. However, our awesome strength is revealed and renewed through an easy choice. Everything we think and anything we can do is better than fear.

Confidence

Empathy

The hurts we suffer are never as great as the damages we can cause. When we use our own feeling as a guide, it is amazing how much more gentle we will become.

Empathy

Endorsement

Just because people are graciously tolerant of us, it does not necessarily mean they endorse our behavior.

Behavior

Engage

Whenever we really focus on an idea both our convictions and doubts will flourish. Neither are worthy of fear. It's better to be engaged in the search than asleep with the thoughtless.

Action

Entropy

Remember when rock music was scandalous, David Letterman was controversial, and marijuana was the devil weed? The passage of time and the movement of history seem to lead many toward an attitude of tolerance. But to really understand the whole of society, we must be kind and sensitive to all. Depending on the issue, growing up for some will always be giving up to others.

Awareness

Fight for Surrender

We can often bring peace to any contentious situation by simply discouraging our ego from joining in. After all, he is loud and rather self-centered.

Humility

First Response

Sometimes when we try to help someone, their unpleasant qualities will become directed towards us. Our healthy reaction should always remain calm because we alone are responsible for entering into their storm. Just like a bomb expert who chooses to put himself in peril, we should never take it personally when someone's troubles explode on us. Contrary to common sense, we know we are in the right place when we have already equipped ourselves to respond to their disaster.

Relationships

Fish Bone

To end neglect, you must first realize the distraction of your own needs. As long as your soul is bereft of peace, contentment, grace and gratitude you can never hand out the loaves and fishes to others.

Unless we all HEAR the words of that famous after-dinner speaker, crumbs will be our lunch and a fish bone will get caught in our throat.

So whenever you feel indigent, just give of yourself to someone else. By feeding him, you are actually filling your own basket.

Neediness

Flick

As you continue at play, always notice your forward motion. Everything you produce is your movie; in progress, scene by scene.

Young actors that think old, and old ones that think even older, yearn for the past. They try to breathe new life into their worn script and begin to see things only as black or white. Nothing is more gone than the flickering images of our past. We may look upon them briefly for comfort or advice, but we must always remember the prime directive:

"We cannot live in or change the past!"

Superman, Jesus, and even Captain Kirk shared this wisdom with us as kids, 2D and in Technicolor.

Just like an old movie theater, there is no fresh air in retrospect. Let's minimize the reruns in our head so that we may enjoy a new opening every night. We all still have "From Here to Eternity". The sun will come out "Tomorrow". And if our story isn't the "Greatest Story Ever Told", it's still pretty good.

In the end, try to play an important role in someone's supporting cast and follow directions more often than you give them.

Life is just a flicker........

Mindfulness

Flow

The best move we can ever make is towards those who appreciate our blessed value, and away from those who do not. "Go with the flow" is more than a common expression. It is a direction from the "Big Guy" with the hose.

Appreciation

23

Fluffy

The purpose of confusion, struggle, disillusionment, and disappointment is to remind us that life is like an old fashioned cake bake off. Everything happens as a test to see if we will rise or fall. Why not take a lesson from the Pillsbury Dough Boy? He has been sifted, mixed up, pounded, shaped, and carefully heated. But in the end he pops out fat, happy, and full of giggles. Always rise! The world needs you fluffy.

Transcendence

Focus

In today's society, the person who can see and do several things at once is much celebrated, but I have always been a "mono-task" type person. I think it has everything to do with my disability because I really can't walk and chew gum at the same time.

If you are like me and are overwhelmed by half done plans and overdue projects, please consider the helpful advice of single-minded focus. It is very quiet and efficient; the time passes quickly and the work is quite intense. But whenever a concentrated effort can bring a job to a quick completion, everything seems a little bit better.

Why not look on a desk or inside a disorganized closet? A wondrous reward awaits for those who can actually see things as they really exist.

Action

Fun

The most fun people to love are those with whom you disagree.

Relationships

Forward Thinking

Most of the wisdom and knowledge we directly use today was left to us by people who are no longer alive. These very words may only have full meaning after I have become compost in Saint Roch Cemetery. So why do we try so hard to contribute to a future society?

Perhaps it's because we are not quite as selfish as we have always been taught. Every day, most people produce something good. When we take the time to realize that many of the things we do are noble and loving, a curious blessing comes over us. We become more willing to give and less willing to consider the reasons.

I have glasses right now because my mama brought me to the eye doctor, and I can read because my daddy paid the tuition years ago.

As you also reflect on the kindness of your parents, please remember the legacy you currently hold for the children of your grandchildren. Love is more than a living joy; it is also our ancestral purpose.

Generosity

Fourth Quarter

Never expect a quarter-horse to win a half mile race. Look around. How many partly finished projects are within easy reach? It might be a handicapped thing, but I think it's important to do all that you can first before you ask for help from anyone.

Using this strategy encourages friends to want to help you and willing participation is always important even if you are not disabled.

Today, design a small activity and finish the job completely. Feeling like a winner is an awesome encouragement! Always track your progress so you can step up in class and win a tougher race next time.

Behavior

Free Hand

We can never fulfill our purpose when anything less is holding us back, and we can never give anything away that we feel we must hold on to. Before we can carry, hold, touch, receive, or bring the highest benefit to anyone, including ourselves, we must have a free hand directed by our will; freely submitted to His.

God's Will

Game Changer

I am an ardent poker player. With my sedentary lifestyle, it is a perfect sport for me. It is a public event in a large room and not an intimate experience over grandma's kitchen table with family. It is often a friendly atmosphere, but the idea is to use patience, math, and observation to relieve your "friend" of his money in a painless way.

The other day while playing poker and watching football, I noticed an old man playing his own little game with the cocktail waitress. He knowingly smiled at me in recognition of our mutual fantasy.

It was at that moment I began to realize just how much of my life had been used up in the investment of games, amusement, entertainment, and fantasy. I know my life would deepen as I shifted from preoccupation to more interest in others, but I also realized that the attraction of self-interest is amazingly strong.

I guess this awareness is a good first step, however. A positive sign that the cards have been shuffled and the game has begun to change is when victory for me must also include a win for others.

Time

Good and Safe

The behavior of some people requires that we pray for them first and befriend them later. It's good for them and safer for us.

Wisdom

Given and Received

Consider the inspiring wisdom of NO! Anyone who cannot properly receive it is seeking an unkind level of personal control. Provide everyone the clarity and confidence that your "yes" really means YES, and your "no" really means NO! Friends, salesmen, children, lovers and pets will all offer their respect once the high value of your true words can be graciously given and received.

Communication

Gold vs. Nuggets

Wisdom, ideas, opportunities, truth, and even love can only be offered. Unused gold is a rock. Cow droppings used wisely help everything grow.

Opportunity

Good Investment

A good friend increases our capacity but never our dependence. The best way to appreciate the investments kind people make in us is to grow beyond our need for them.

Friendship

Good – No Good

I once heard this from a guy who held the elevator door open for me, "If we are not good to each other, then we are no good for anything else." His simple comment and gesture uplifted me more than the elevator ride.

Relationships

Grit

Absolutely everything takes longer than we think it should. I know because I am writing this over a bowl of crunchy instant grits!

Patience

Hands and Heart

Words are just a magic spell that can be easily mixed and quickly changed. But it takes hands and heart, mind and muscle to actually produce anything of value. Without substance and action, our words can scarcely move the air.

Action

Hang Out

Nothing can benefit us more than maturity, awareness, and discipline. I always enjoy hanging out with people who help me feel safe but it's even more fun when they share all that they know.

Associations

Heroic Choice

The greatest indication we are living a heroic life is when we can forgive everybody, everywhere, on an ongoing active basis. This is particularly important when the hurt is still fresh and trying to cause us harm. It's easier to forgive when the infraction stops. But when we can forgive even before people hurt us and with the full knowledge that they will probably do so again, then we know that a new courage has begun to define us. This transcendent choice is a daily chance for growth when we decide to become more fully engaged with life.

Along with forgiveness, we must also allow for and even encourage a wide avenue for reconciliation. This is the true measure of any heroic choice and only heroes will make it.

Forgiveness

Hold

A healthy spirit requires freedom from constriction and addictions of every kind. Mature encouragement needs unimpeded access to an honest heart. So we must remain clear of anything or anyone who might try to hold us up or pull us down. It may seem ironic, but when we become secured to a narrower path, opportunities increase as our desires find control.

Let's stay at peace, and remain comfortable within ourselves. Our higher attitude will help us prevail whenever we are tempted to become less. We must always be willing to help others in the hope our help will be properly received. But we must also recognize that our good intentions can sometimes become unguided missiles when misused by misguided people.

God's Will

Impression

The true measure of a successful manipulator is their strong desire to seduce us and our open willingness to participate. The evil of this connivance is that as long as they possess a hold on us we will never know about it.

Before we surrender anything to anyone we must watch for flags and believe the warning from our friends. The entire purpose of a first impression is to prevent a lasting scar or a deeper mark.

Manipulation

Inside My Kitten

Our specific happiness is a gift that we can give to everyone we know and everyone we can touch. Therefore, it is never selfish to do things that make us happy in a healthy way. Happiness is the spiritual gift that is the most fun to share. God puts it inside of every kitten, puppy, and child just so we will have a never-ending supply.

Self-esteem

It

When we really don't want "it", the universe will honor our choice. We will never have "it" or get "it" This applies to everything.

Choice

Jealousy

When you want things that other people have, it could be that you just lost count of your own cool stuff. Once you learn to expand the experience of being you, it's easy to see your own abundance.

Gratitude is the fine art of becoming so thankful that you can even appreciate when someone is jealous of you.

Gratitude

Jump into the Basket

Run from those who show you disrespect, because they insult His Spirit inside. But run even faster from those who teach you how to lose respect for them, because His Spirit has left them completely.

Now from the safety of distance, offer them honor and respect as an example of your gifts. No one can take from you or give to you what they don't have for themselves. Love, dignity and respect are exactly like the loaves and fishes. Every time you give some away, more will jump into your basket.

Respect

Kind Of

Public discussion is best understood through careful observation. Notice that the first people to speak are frequently those who know nothing. Then they are quickly followed by those who feel that they know it all. But the most unstable group in any debate are those people who really did not listen in the first place and only mildly comprehend. Always be cautious around the "know it almost!" They are often the most vocal because they are the least prepared.

As Alexander Pope said, "A little learning is a dangerous thing."

Wisdom

Kinship

A friend suggested that I judge people only after I completely understand them. When I realized that I could never meet that requirement, I began to have a deeper appreciation for our similarities and the value of acceptance.

Judgment

Laugh at Foolishness

Angry thoughts never lead to constructive purposes. The best in us needs the calm, balance, and emotional control that anger needs to upset. When we can laugh at foolishness rather than become more disturbed by it, evil loses its hold over us. No one is more effective in a difficult situation than a warm hearted person with a good sense of humor.

Self-control

Lend - Lease

Whenever someone lends you their ear, at least say something intelligent or give it right back!

Communication

Loop

It's easy to get hung up on all the drama and disappointments in life and allow them to play as a loop inside our mind. But when we get stuck on review, we can miss the best part of the story.

Painful experiences will always create a deeper awareness in us, and this new perception can help generate a strength and compassion so we can better understand the next difficult experience.

Life is full of pitfalls, traps, and snares. Try to develop the courage and forbearance to avoid them and never allow anything to spoil the forward motion of your movie.

Attitude

Mindfulness

This moment. Do you ever really enjoy it? No, not the last instant when you began to read this note. Right now! Breathe!

Notice the air fill your lungs and the movement of your chest. Listen carefully. That is your heart beating and your ears working. Close your eyes and step inside yourself. Forget to think and do, and honor the gift of stillness. Living at this moment and inside of it, you are a complete....... Human........ Being.......

Diligence

More Gentle Judgment

One of the best decisions we can make is the daily choice to become less judgmental. Isn't this the proper response to the fact that we all must face judgment someday? Many Christians suffer from a mild form of arrogance similar to that displayed in the game of Monopoly when a player holds the "get out of jail free" card.

The worst arrogance of all is spiritual arrogance. I know some of my friends may consider this note harsh because it reveals a big secret contained inside some churches, seminaries, bible studies, and hearts, but my personal experience speaks to this truth.

Within Americanized Christianity, I am not suggesting an increased tolerance that our faith and standards cannot permit. What I am suggesting instead is a heightened compassion birthed within the spirit of the formerly incarcerated towards those currently in jail.

Mother Teresa picked the bugs off of Muslims, Hindus, Christians, Jews, and atheists. Can our nonjudgmental hearts ever grow large enough to do the same?

Judgment

Measure

The best measure of a person and his wealth are the things that don't possess him.

Gratitude

Monument

If we had the bronze, cast iron, granite, hammer and chisel, wouldn't we create our own grand statutes if we could?

It is a fun illusion to find some space, cut a slab, and trim the words of remembrance. But reality has a way of diminishing our ego and revealing its forgeries. Inside our mind greatness takes only a few moments to fabricate. But the truth reminds us of a very different scenario. To become a noble hero on a green horse, we need to develop more than just a brass heart. We need to build a life with care, mindful of our stature. Only then will our monumental efforts begin to have any historic value.

Achievement

Nobility

If we are truly wise and they are truly humble, we can look past a person's frailty to see their strength instead. When we notice their inner nobility we are actually helping them back on the horse.

Encouragement

Nurture

The seeds of greatness are not sowed on a battlefield or inside a boardroom, classroom, or nursery. They first sprout within our fertile spiritual imagination and are warmed and watered every time we take full responsibility for our actions. We can never lead others to health and growth until they have first been nurtured within us.

Responsibility

Offered

Wisdom, ideas, opportunities, truth, and even love can only be offered; and they remain useless until accepted.

Gratitude

One Direction

Sometimes we can be fooled by appearance and direction. If we intend to walk a mile but turn back halfway, we have still accomplished our goal. Even a step back has an important purpose and lesson.

Guidance

Only

Make certain when you tell people of the things you need, they don't control the only supply.

Generosity

Open and Shut

A great friend has an open heart, mind, and wallet but also knows when to shut his mouth.

Friendship

Oprah's Dogs

Imagine our life if people treated us as well as Oprah's dogs and we did the same for them.

Kindness

Parade

Never allow anyone to disrupt your parade because they are so deluded with their own. Here is the deal and here is the truth! They might sing the words of righteousness or seem to wear the clothes of humility, but the word "ME" is printed all over their costume. This isn't news and this isn't new.

Get out of their second line and proceed down your own narrow path. Cast your bread, your net, and your lot; assured that wherever His light is, their darkness isn't! Always distribute your gifts freely as if you are on the king's float on Mardi Gras day because you are!

Righteousness

Pardon

Whenever we try to find fault in others it's not much of a challenge. So for fun, why not search for their goodness instead? It helps them grow and pardons us.

Judgment

Piglets, Pearls, and Puppies

I wonder what would happen if we continued to offer kindness to others even when it was not well received? Of course, there is great wisdom in not casting our goodness before swine, or feeding a mad dog until it turns on us. But what if we noticed that all people are just piglets and puppies looking for warmth?

When you get a chance, try bouncing a pearl of wisdom off the head of a sad person today. It's just a new opportunity to demonstrate love. They might just turn to you rather than on you as they discover a new friend. But if they still seem emotionally traumatized or confined, just reach through the bars of their cage and rub their ears.

Kindness

Plaque

In my hometown, many schools, roads, building, and bridges are named after people I actually knew. It's quite disconcerting because I never really thought any of them were a "Thomas Jefferson" type. Soon I began to think about how I would like to be remembered. I decided that my next personal goal would be to try to live my life worthy of an inscription in the end.

Somehow I think I would get up earlier and try a bit harder. I have never really thought it was appropriate for a man to polish his own plaque. But there would be a certain satisfaction if I was so kindly remembered that my rather unusual surname was spelled correctly in the mausoleum and someone actually noticed.

Achievement

Point

From a small frustration to a major disaster, both are easier to endure with a point shift in our thinking. The same rainstorm that brings lightning and fire to the forest also brings with it much needed rain.

Our view tends to be myopic especially when it comes to the things we want or think we have earned. The disappointing truth is that although the world does revolve, it doesn't really revolve around us.

Whenever we enjoy cheap clothes, we need to think about the far off child labor behind them. And the next time our team loses by a missed field goal, let's think about the kicker's mama crying at home.

Empathy

Propriety

Whenever we criticize others aren't we actually reinforcing our values and trying to impose them? Why not just choose to love regardless of changeable feelings or variation in behavior? After all, we can never really control the actions of other people, nor should we try. Instead, let us imagine the benefit we could bring to life if our reaction were always confident, calm, peaceful, and loving. Growth is realizing that the change we seek in our brother is actually ours to make. Propriety always begins at home.

Growth

Quality

The two best qualities anyone can possess are a good sense of humor and an even better sense of seriousness.

Attitude

Radio Head

Today it's easier to recognize that not all notes make good music and many words still lack wisdom. In order to live a harmonious life, we must reduce the static from all the disturbed and disquieted voices. I find it is helpful to think of some friends like overpaid talk show hosts. As soon as they lose their entertainment value, I ask them to tone it down. If that does not work, then I try to tune them out. Finally, if necessary, I purposely turn them off. Unless we kindly choose to surrender our peaceful life to ignorant bombast, it's rarely helpful to become someone's sounding board or captive audience.

Communication

Rally

The internet has taught some from this generation the art of anonymous cruelty. I call on my generation of peace to dust off your bell-bottoms and once again become notorious for your love. Rallies, signage, megaphones, and speeches are much less effective now. But you may still be able to inspire the young from your couch with a keyboard, spell-check, and a little hippie wisdom.

Action

Rant vs. Reason

Every night a new rant, rage, and rave is brought into my house via a cable subscription. It might be a new subject, but it always seems to be the same red-faced, talking head. I often wonder how they ever keep an audience. As soon as their respect for their guest goes out the door, my reason to listen to them goes out the window.

Communication

Reason For Spring

What is lacking in your life? If you are anything like me, it's not the many problems but rather their creative solutions. Here are a few questions that I have asked myself:

"Am I actively engaged with a church, family, friends, finance, health, and God? Do I tend to learn more each day or care less? Have I surrendered to the flow in life or just given up to defeat? Am I well-organized and at peace, or is every day just another whirlwind of aimless activity? Are my motives clean and do I seek to inspire others rather than try to manipulate or command them? "

The truth is that miraculous solutions rarely come to those who strive for less and they will never come to those who are too busy. Lazy people will not know a miracle when it comes, and busy people will never notice when the water becomes wine, walked upon; or parted. After much thought, I came up with a few ideas to share:

1.   Try praying. It's so easy even the indolent can do it.

2.   Pay closer attention to everything. (Prayer will be your guide.)

3.   Become more grateful. Be grateful about the good stuff, and accepting of the hard stuff because EVERYTHING is a gift; though the wrapping and ribbon changes every day.

Perhaps you have a difficult problem today? What great news! Unwrap it. Enjoy it. And overcome it. The next special delivery is always just down the street.

In the vast emptiness between void and creation, only positive activity really fits in. It is the reason for IS. It is the definition for ALL. And it is why God is the: " I AM."

Attitude

Real Genius

The worst in us often sparks the discovery of our best. A real genius is anyone who learns how to use the things that used to hold him back as motivation to push himself and others forward.

Motivation

Recruit

In the same way the world needs firefighters, it needs optimists. An optimist understands the awesome destructive power of pessimism and he needs to stand against it. Every day an optimist must welcome new recruits to his cause because he knows his example will persuade them.

Optimism

41

Reduce the Pressure

The most creative way to reduce the pressure of need is to become more grateful for all that we already have. Gratitude is an amazing creature. It expands our treasure, gives us keener eyesight, and always makes room for more blessings. The moment we become friends with gratitude, we realize that we really deserve it.

Gratitude

Regardless

Before any experience, we can either hope for the best or expect the worst. However, we can always predetermine our own success when hope remains within us regardless of the outcome.

Attitude

Restore

The next time you replace a light bulb or reconstitute some orange juice please remember that you can also do the same with your perspective. Positive thoughts are just as valid as negative ideas with one important difference. Positive speculation creates a better experience under every circumstance.

For a richer life, why not start looking at everything in a more positive light? At the very least it will make your failures easier to see.

Optimism

Sack Full of Puppies

I have a most gracious and generous young friend. He is always respectful, and especially humble. He receives a compliment with grace and demands so little in return because he already knows he possesses everything.

Many people I know require daily calls, texts, or e-mails because insecurities consume them. They demand respect for their time and opinions, but they lack a simple grace and empathy for others. Sadly as their ego grows, their actions cause them to possess less.

My friend is one of 13 brothers and sisters. When you connect with him or any of them, joy fills their voice. They uplift your soul and make you feel like Santa has come on Christmas Day with a sack full of puppies! They are always happy to see you no matter the pressures of their own life because they know this secret:

"Treat all people like a king or a queen because they are actually more important than you are."

When we can make a noble connection to others, it gives more than it takes away because we are actually connecting to God Himself. Therefore, it is important that we never become so involved with ourselves that we become unavailable to others. Plus here is an added bonus prize: "Whenever we make ourselves available to give, we are also opening the flood gate to receive!"

Generosity

Sweep

If you feel yourself being pounded by a reckless opinion, stand firm to your convictions with a calm and more precise wisdom. Whenever anything needs to be aggressively pushed, there is normally a good reason for its resistance. Beware of any heady statement or bold assurance without the weight of evidence. And never allow your common sense the sweep of pure emotion.

Wisdom

Salesman

Some people start out as a shepherd to our path but soon become a clever guide to the ditch. Be wary of anyone who smiles too broad, talks too smooth, or cares a little too much. Such behavior is the first warning sign of a master manipulator. If such conduct remains unchecked it can lead to a dangerous dependency. Self-respect and self-sufficiency are always a better choice.

Every decision we make reveals the true measure of us. When we seek to control others by the power of our personality, we know for certain God is not in charge. Our darkest side glows when our ego remains disobedient. All human tragedy begins as a lack of humility.

Sensitivity to God's voice and submission to His Will is our only protection from the super salesman; especially when he may secretly live, work, and sleep inside of us.

Manipulation

Satisfied

Sometimes it's unfair to demand the highest levels of cooperation from people who are so similar to us. The truth is our expectations are most often ethereal and possess the same certainty as a birthday wish. Even our best friends can only give us what they already have and most people will only give us what they really want to.

So when you are offered part of the 7 loaves and fishes today as your daily bread, be satisfied and don't demand a house salad, more coffee, and a big dessert!

Peace

Second

Let's be honest. For most of us our reach only includes the people and things that are important to us. Just like kids on a ball team, when we require someone to make an extra effort before we notice them, we are not really their friend.

This kind of selfishness can easily expand from "out of sight, out of mind" to become "out of mind, out of existence."

In our world today, it seems humanity's biggest interests involve the accumulation of money, power, influence, security and comfort. We must face the dark truth that when we neglect people, we do so on purpose, with purpose, using our personal power to choose.

Why is it so hard for us to extend our reach beyond our personal desires? Actually, it's not that difficult when we use a little creative imagination. The moment we actually decide to make the needs of others more important, we will want to spend more time and resources in service to them. Our power comes from the happiness we can bring as we fulfill a higher purpose. Over time and with practice service to others can actually be a first rate experience.

Unselfishness

Self

To be real, our self-perception must remain steady. Credibility helps everyone. It is the source of all true power because it is God being God and us remaining true to Him. Without authenticity, God isn't and neither are we.

Authenticity

Shot

Present a painful truth in a gentle way. People need a shot in the arm more than a shot in the face.

Advice

Should

Of course, I believe one person can and should make a difference but only when I am in complete agreement with them!

Behavior

Significance

I grew up in a time when the first law of significance stated that the wisest advice would always find its way through inferior noise and conflicting traffic just because it came from more successful thought and disciplined behavior.

But now that the internet has given us a global society of free expression, it is even more difficult to stand apart. Sadly, the perceptive and enlightened seem to share equal access with the blind and uninformed. Today everyone has more than an opinion. They have a desktop publisher and entry into a worldwide network.

Don't despair and don't give up. The course is just a little more crowded, but the practice remains the same. When you work hard every day to become better, you still become a challenger to the people in front and an aspiration for those behind. Even with all the advances in technology there has been little change in the race for those who want to make a significant effort.

Behavior

Similarity

Hassles more easily dissipate once we can lessen our ego and focus attention on our brother. The graciousness we have helped create may then encourage him to have a similar attitude towards us.

Love

Single

As my thoughts coalesce on to this page, I am reminded of the joys of a single minded focus. It's really true that most people can only do one thing at a time and juggling is a rare and highly developed skill.

Just for the benefit of a new experience, try turning off the TV as you work on your phone or computer. Isolate your attention and privatize your powers for just a few moments. Congratulations! Your quality, substance, and output have all just increased!

Mindfulness

Snake

As the Indians used to say, be wary of anyone who speaks with a forked tongue. It allows them to talk from both sides of their mouth at the same time.

Authenticity

Spectacle

I was taught the value of single-minded thought and independence in the '60's and 70's, but the truth is rugged individualism does not work well with a physical disability. In fact, the best definition for a disability is a dependence of some kind. No one who is psychologically healthy enjoys dependence, but it is an easy trap to fall into when a handicapping condition spans a lifetime.

The key to helping any person in a wheelchair is rather simple. Just ask them what they need and try to allow them the ability to maintain their dignity. The common belief that most people with a disability do not want to be helped is false. We just don't want your small kindness to become a lavish expression or a Mardi Gras Parade!

Help

Spin

On the chance, you find yourself spinning your wheels through life, try looking to a person in a wheelchair for some practical advice.

We squarely face every situation forward and in an upright position. We also avoid most rocky situations, so you will rarely find us in a tight squeeze or inclined to fight an uphill battle. Our normal viewpoint is on a cushion of air, so we almost never drag our feet or pull other people down.

The most important lesson to learn from us is to always keep trying! Be patient and good people will open doors for you. Good traction is sometimes difficult to find so just dig in and muscle through. Quite often an unseen force is just behind ready to offer a push!

Motivation

Steam

Because memories fade as history passes, there is a much better way to expedite your aspirations. Turn your life into an active verb rather than a tired and worn descriptive adjective. When your daily life is in pursuit of a live and progressive dream there is no time for regret or reminiscence.

The quickest way to invigorate your life is to follow the advice of the famous Nike commercial and just do it!

Motivation

Step Over

Many people love to overreact and give negative power to life experiences. The experience itself is neither positive nor negative. In your parade, some people will always dump on you like an unruly horse trying to slow your progress. Train yourself to step over, around, or even through distasteful situations and never allow anything or anyone to cause you to miss a beat.

Moving Forward

Support

Similar to the behavior of a sand pit or sinkhole, it is impossible to take a firm moral stand supported on unholy grounds.

Morality

Switch

Just as important as the light itself, is a friend who can help you turn the switch.

Inspiration

Tag

I often think back on the wonderful times we had as kids and the great rapport we seemed to have with each other at school or when we played outside. Then I realized that there were no real reasons we could not try to relive those good memories today.

Let's search the profiles of our current Facebook friends and try to fulfill a small desire or an unmet need. Just for a day, why not tag a good friend and make their day extra special? We are essentially the same great kids we were in our khaki uniforms or gym shorts except now we can drive and some of us have a few extra bucks.

Friendship

Take It Easy

Difficulties are always an opportunity to graduate to a higher level. Rather than just endure them, we can actually grow to enjoy them. The best life we can have faces challenges head on and searches for ways to have fun in everything. Surprisingly, this is an easy task when we can continue to smile as we happily grit our teeth.

Transcendence

The Best Gift

The best gift we can ever give someone is the gift of our maturity. Personal maturity is built like a brick wall; one correct decision adjacent to another. Sometimes we must experience a lack of wisdom repeatedly until the blessed bricks fall on our head. When this happens we should thank God for the quake and His gift of a headache because He has given us another memorable experience!

Maturity

Them

A healthy life begins the moment we realize it is not at all about them but rather our reaction to them. A cool and breezy attitude has always been one of the best qualities of a Saint, so it is helpful to develop a good attitude now if we ever hope to become one.

Peace

Token

Tomorrow imagine the good you could bring with just a little extra conscience service. A ride, a meal or a helping hand may seem like a worthless token but every kindness has tremendous value. When you empower your thoughts with your hands and feet, you can actually create a living miracle.

Service

Topic

Today there seems to be an amplified interest in more diverse topics as reported by the trending media. This new phenomenon is somewhat disturbing because the process is both relentless and arbitrary. It now seems that important issues are less separate from feature stories and other expeditious silliness.

Please join with me in search of more salient content to confront our problems as we try to inspire society.

I don't have anything against movie stars and their arrest records. I just don't want them to dominate my higher thoughts and news feeds.

Communications

Touch

The popular idea that we cannot make someone feel anything is false. It is a physiological fact that when someone touches us, we both experience a similar sensitivity.

When we need people to be more careful, gentle, and considerate towards us, we must first offer the same gift to them. It's ironic but whatever we really need in life seems to come to us just at the moment we give it away.

Sowing and Reaping

Tower

On 24-hour news TV, doesn't it always seem like the dawn of a new political season?

I personally don't care if someone is a Republican, Democrat, Libertarian, Independent, or Socialist. If he or she is smart, kind, authentic, courageous, effective, and spiritual, these qualities trump all others and they tower above the rest. The sad truth, however, is that money, power, effort, and time is wasted when it is spent by anyone of questionable character.

Opinion

Trespass

Notice the focus, time, energy, and effort we invest in those who have trespassed against us, yet our own trespasses barely receive an honorable mention.

Awareness

Two and Four

Sometimes our stupidity will allow people to do things to us, but our wisdom must always inspire us to continue to do things for them. Life is chock full of constrictions that become double blessing.

Action

Twinkle

For those who wish to be fully human: "Eyes without tears are dead; for it is the tears in our eyes that cause them to twinkle."

Compassion

Unless

We can't teach wisdom unless we are already wise and we can't inspire others unless we are first inspirational. And we can't love anyone until we learn to love ourselves.

Awareness

Up and Away

No person or event can take our happiness from us unless we choose to give it up or away.

Influence

Value

Invest most of your time with people you value and the rest of your time becoming a value to them.

Self-respect

Victim

I was born in 1954 two months early, eager for life, but not completely formed. Therefore, Cerebral Palsy has always been my most obvious and notable challenge. Fortunately, it has only physically affected my balance and posture; allowing my speech and most of my intelligence to remain.

In daily therapy from the late '50's until the early '70's we were referred to as crippled children who were victims of Cerebral Palsy. Our dingy little clinic was not a happy place and for us as kids, there was nothing inspirational about it. We were disciplined through pain and always encouraged to just accept our situation. In this environment, the seeds of my personality were developed.

Since I could hear and speak, I became the interpreter for my more handicapped friends. I purposely drew fire away from the weaker kids by learning that if I could distract the therapist and make them laugh, they would make it easier when it came to physical or psychological punishment.

I wasn't overly wise, courageous, motivated or ingenious. I was just a little boy who wanted to take his braces off and play.

Attitude

Whack

A vital quality for a happy life is balance. It works well for diets, checkbooks, relationships, wheel alignments, and mental states. I wonder if it would throw our world out of whack if we recklessly tried to seek it, teach it, and possess it?

Balance

When People Are A Pain

A good way for a friend not to become a pain to us is to try to remain a pleasure for them. The attributes of patience have an interesting feature. They still provide a deep personal reward to us even when others cannot reciprocate.

Friendship

Who - What - Where

Weakness and strength have a few things in common. They thrive on the power and attention we give them. "Where are your thoughts? Who is your source? And what are your choices today?"

Attitude

2

PRESSING FORWARD

Perpetual Motion

When we finally face the person we are, we will think better about ourselves. When we think better about ourselves, the person we are will always want to catch up.

Awareness

Actually

When we think we are so good it's actually too bad.

Behavior

A Thought

What is imagination without action to realize it? It is just something to think about.

Action

All and More

It's difficult to focus on all that we have while still searching for more. Need and greed are cultural blinders and they often overshadow our gifts. Let us give serenity to a hungry world by receiving two of life's greatest hidden treasures; gratitude and contentment. As the old song reminds us:

"Let there be peace on earth and let it begin with me."

Gratitude

All Wisdom Is Noise

Everybody talks too much. Without integrity words are wind and wisdom is noise.

Integrity

Anticipation

Whatever comes provides growth. We even have the power within to turn fear into anticipation. After all, as long as we seek proper guidance, what are we actually afraid of?

Growth

Arrow

Life is like cupid's arrow. When we concentrate on who is giving us the shaft, we miss the glorious heartfelt point!

Attitude

Backwards

When I was a child the President was always older and wiser, social commentary was rendered by Eric Sevareid and Edward R. Murrow and Whoopi Goldberg and Rosie O'Donnell were just funny kids. Reality TV showed actual war and when you saw "Dancing with the Stars" it always included Fred Astaire, Ginger Rogers, and Gene Kelly because they were actual stars and they really could dance!

I realize time has moved on and we live in more a aggressive and progressive world. But one of the best ways to understand our current direction and location is to be able to look back and use our memory to help guide us better today.

Experience

Advice

Good advice is often ruined by too much instruction, correction, and criticism. We all believe that the people we advise would be much better off if they were more like us. So let's offer them this encouragement instead: "Everybody who tries often will make plenty mistakes. It is the universal law of math and physics."

When you see their eyes widen, you will realize that you have just given them the right advice.

Encouragement

Affect

Forgiveness does not pretend we were not assaulted. It just asks us to remain calm, willing, and undeterred in the pursuit of our next encounter. Through grace and forgiveness, the most effective people manage to remain unaffected. They continue to try, never hold a grudge, and seem to attract the most amazing friends.

Forgiveness

Balance

As a healthy instrument for God's love, relentless care for our brother must always remain balanced by an unselfish love for ourselves. When we finally realize we are His most cherished possession, He then will allow us to watch out for the rest of His kids.

Self-respect

Battle as Entertainment

The most difficult people to deal with are those who must prove they are always right. Whatever the issue, kindness and respect for them will help our cause. Some people just love self-expression and personal conflict is their form of entertainment.

By tolerating a different opinion with confidence, we already stand apart from most. Then from a higher platform, curious people may listen to our words, join in the discussion, and eventually share our viewpoint just because of our calmer and more mature attitude.

Transcendence

Beacon

Today in many coastal communities the lighthouse is the oldest structure still standing. During difficult times, just picture one of these beautiful markers in your mind. Calm down, climb the stairs, and flip the switch. As you look out for ways to guide others, help will regularly come around to also show you the way.

Guidance

Become

Become the person you wish others were, so that when they can't show up, at least you can still enjoy the company.

Growth

Begun

The moment we can view an ordeal as an adventure, we have already proven to the adversity we can overcome it.

Transcendence

Being

Giving too much power to the past or having too much expectation for the future can really mess up your day. You are no longer there to actually enjoy the things you have done and you have yet to realize the impact of anything you will do. Everything that you can influence is completely contained in the present.

So when things are not going well, rather than seeking comfort in the illusions of memory or anticipation just stop and actively feel sorry for yourself for a little while. It will allow you to realize that you have a friend that currently understands because he shares in your footprint and shoe size. A daily funeral is a great idea because you can move on to a better place and healthier circumstances seconds after you have sung the last hymn.

Let's liberate ourselves from history and relieve ourselves from wishes; so we can create a happier life. There is tremendous joy in just being present in the moment.

Mindfulness

Belief

You exist because God believes in you and your belief in Him verifies His judgment!

Faith

Bench

We empty our lives and damage good hearts whenever we judge others from the sidelines.

A better life comes to those who simply try. When the team is chosen and the game begins, only team players rise from the benches that harsh critics used to occupy.

Judgment

Better Purpose

The deeper purposes of faith and love are concealed from us until we don't have any.

Need

Blue Tooth

I can remember a much happier time when a blackberry was grandma's best pie offering and every neighborhood kid would proudly show her their blue tooth when they finished. I can only imagine my grandma's thoughts if she were here to experience today.

Progress

Bluff

My mama once told me she read this quote in a magazine. "Be careful that you have a great understanding of how people operate before you seek to operate on them."

Of all my life experiences; 16 years of formal education, 15 years in politics, Christian conversion, continuous physical disability, books, cable, the internet, hurricanes, and all my relationships, nothing has educated me better than the complex game of poker.

More truth, lies, passion, cruelty, kindness, and character can be revealed at the rail of a poker table than on the rail of any church altar in the world. In poker, it's easy to determine how people secretly reveal themselves. This is known as "a tell". In real life the same skill serves. It helps to show the real truth behind a winning smile, a false friendship, or a disingenuous handshake. Without authenticity, a man has nothing because he actually is nothing. Every aspect of a person's character eventually comes to light when we can train ourselves to pay closer attention. The game of poker has taught me that better choices always lead to more winning combinations and closer observation is a gift available to all of us.

Winners never bluff through life. Smart people can see through a fake easily and the eye in the sky has a clear picture of everything else.

Authenticity

Bounce

Sometimes the loudest words are unspoken. Jesus proved before Pilate and the Sanhedrin that selective silence can be very effective. Silence does not necessarily mean agreement or approval. But age and experience teach us that anyone who contributes to quiet in a heated discussion is most often the true leader of the group.

The moment you suspect your ideas will bounce over the other guy's head, it's best to end the useless shouting match.

Communication

Bug

Exactly as it does in nature, whenever we shine our light, it attracts some people that bug us. No worries. It gives us an opportunity to improve our patience, and it affirms the necessity of our light. Without irritation, we would not see the value of our illumination. Be careful who you brush off. Even bugs can serve a useful purpose.

Patience

Carry a Burden

I once read a similar story on the internet concerning stress management and I would like to expand on it here.

A physics professor raised a glass of water and asked, "How heavy is this glass of water?" Answers called out ranged from 20g to 500g. The lecturer replied, "The absolute weight doesn't really matter. It only depends on how long you try to hold it."

If we hold it for a minute, that's not a problem.
If we hold it for an hour, we will have an ache in our right arm.
If we hold it for a day, we will have to call an ambulance.

In each case, it's the same weight, but the longer we hold it, the heavier it becomes.

And that's the way it is with stress management. If we carry our burdens all the time, sooner or later, as the burden becomes increasingly heavy, we won't be able to carry on. As with the glass of water, we have to put it down for a while and rest before holding it again. When we're refreshed, we can carry on with the burden.

So, before we return home tonight, we must put the burden of work down. We must not carry it home to our loving dog, kids, spouse or goldfish. So what! We can pick it up tomorrow.

Put down anything that may be a burden to you right now! Don't pick it up again until after you've rested. Pet your dog, mate, and kids, and feed your goldfish. Breathe!

Relaxation

Cast

At a time of "rejection-ist" policies and perfectionist ideas, it is always better to cast your light rather than throw some shade.

Optimism

Catch Up

People can only act or react up to their level of awareness. Empathy is the art of sharing our emotional understanding so that they may catch up with us or we can catch up to them.

Empathy

Certainty

When people can count on your word, even "NO" becomes a welcomed answer.

In an insincere world, certainty is valued. It may seem ironic, but people of good faith rarely talk about their promises. They are careful when they speak because they know that their character is formed by keeping their word.

Character

Church

Here's the church.
There's the steeple.

The real message is missed,
by most of the people.

Awareness

Class

A group of my friends were talking about politics recently and one of us said: "It would be a tragedy if so and so were elected."
Then someone chimed in: "It's always a tragedy when the person we don't happen to agree with is elected."

No media source or single personality is the fount of all wisdom. Personal class is the ability to enjoy and respect a perspective that is different from our own. And maturity is the wisdom to learn from it.

Wisdom

Come and Go

Some people find it "hard to stay" around people who are too optimistic because it is difficult for them to keep up. An important part of friendship is trying to understand where someone has come from. If a companion does not have your abilities, experience, and disposition try to be gracious to them anyway.

Everyone in the Jesus crew had a unique temperament, and all but one cooperated. In a lifetime of change, all types of people will come and go. It is vital to develop a seasonal attitude of trust and confidence with people. Make it easy for friends to come into your life and make it even easier for them when it is time for them to go.

Relationships

Critical

It is always better to encourage our friends rather than to criticize them. We may really need them someday if we find ourselves in critical condition.

Encouragement

67

Credential

Before we can offer deep understanding and wise psychiatric counseling we should always consider our actual credentials first. Although we possess our own experience and love to give advice, a quiet prayer is always more effective than an inadequate opinion.

I remember all the weird persuasions and subtle duplicity that I have endured throughout my life and I now use them as a guideline for a more careful private practice. When we can step aside and allow for more qualified professional help, our humility can flower and provide authentic support for our friends during a difficult time.

Opinion

Dance

The best gift you can ever give a friend is a gracious reception. Whenever you see him trying hard to tap dance for you, love is helping him lace up his shoes.

Grace

Dead Weight

You can tell at his wake when a man used his life to manipulate others. The receptionist, the funeral director, and the lady who served the donuts will all struggle to lift his casket into the hearse.

Manipulation

Distance

Whenever we are unkind to anyone who does not look or think like us, we are not only creating a distance from them. We have created exactly the same distance from God. It is because at that moment and in that moment He also does not look or think like us.

Relationships

Divorce

When someone is suffering from a heartache that they think we have caused, it may be better to just walk away rather than try to fix something we don't understand. We should offer them our blessings, and forgiveness, but we should not poke at their resentments as they are trying to mend. True love is not about our needs but theirs, and it does not insist on its own way. It's always good to keep a wide avenue open for reconciliation, but we should not require any condition from them for a more distant love. Love conquers all even from farther away.

Moving Forward

Dizzy

Maturity comes the moment we realize all that we have can easily replace all that we think we need. We must stop the race our ego and the spirit of the world will never allow us to win. It's always more fun to watch others race from the shade of the winner's circle. A dizzy rat may even stop by for a cool drink that only we can offer.

Need

Driver

As a guy in a wheelchair, I have been pushed around a lot. I have enjoyed the ease, the ride, and the companionship, but where I went was not always my idea. To get anywhere we must push ourselves beyond the disabilities we all have or sometimes invent. Even in a wheelchair it is always more fun to be the driver rather than someone's captivated passenger.

Motivation

EMT

Our most powerful resource is a positive attitude, but we should never become so cavalier in our approach that we lose our empathy for the people we try to serve. Optimism and compassion should work together like EMT 's on a dangerous rescue mission.

Before we can lift others to the anticipation and trust of cloud 9, we must gently prepare them and make sure they are ready on cloud 8.

Empathy

Either Way

A good life can be as simple as this: share your peace when you can feel it and remain at peace with yourself especially when you cannot.

Peace

Eye

Wherever we are and whoever we choose to be, nothing remains hidden forever. All things are noted, recorded and measured. Our cat or dog is not our only audience.

Awareness

First

The first act of maturity is to easily receive for ourselves the hard instructions we love to give to others.

Guidance

Float

Whenever you happen to have negative or selfish thoughts, remember they don't have to define your flight. They just might be the temporary sandbags attached to your balloon to test the strength of your gondola or they could be the over-inflated opinion you have of yourself. Cut, float, and rise!

Transcendence

Follow-ship

Whenever we play follow the leader, the best way to inspire them, is to create them.

Leadership

Gap

In the space between desire and action, most of our life is used up and wasted. We must learn to bridge this gulf with tiny steps so that failure, loss, and disappointment will not notice our movement. Once on the other side of wishful thinking, we can then surrender to success and allow it to provide some momentum.

You have an urge right now. Use it to shift your attention if only to stir your coffee. As you encourage the caffeine to satisfy its mission, notice how even small changes can harden your resolve into a progressive path.

The truth is that there are always large gaps in our imagination that only activity can fulfill.

Action

Gentle Heart

Treat all people as if they have a gentle heart, because at least to themselves, and their mama, they do.

Behavior

Hard to Face

Rather than a cause for disruption, difficulty can be trained to become a productive friend. Any struggle can work hard to enhance our credibility as we continue to offer encouragement right in its face.

Encouragement

Hemingway

"In order to write about life, first you must live it." --

Ernest Hemingway

Sadly, for many, his suicide is much better remembered than his life or his awesome writings.

I guess he had the last word because he felt sick and empty towards the end, but he might have had even more to say if only he had allowed himself to wake up the next day to realize the sun also rises.

Hope

Heresy

In a world filled with overrated arrogance, there is a lot to be said for understated elegance. Measured tones and crafted words are rarely used today, but they can help the heart to listen. The only thing that really matters is sound advice that can be well understood and graciously received.

Communication

Hidden Treasure

There is a treasure in the pain we must experience alone and value in the words we cannot express. They deepen our substance and advance our ability to feel.

Love

Hero

Choose travel companions that offer help rather than an unnecessary burden and become the same good porter for them. A good friend clears our path and helps us become a better explorer. In return, we can help them develop their own heroic qualities.

Friendship

Hint

Here's a help to maximize any experience. Find a way to make it more enjoyable. Sure life can be difficult with all its hidden challenges. But everything can be made more interesting by creative invention. Our mind and spirit are great playmates when we can inspire them to find amusement in every situation.

"WHO DAT" say can beat us when we decide to make life more fun!

*(Note: I am from New Orleans and a big Saints fan)

Attitude

High and Low

Continually seek ways to love without regard for a lesser response. Our higher choices are never diminished by their lower reactions.

Attitude

Honest Man

If a person chooses honesty he would be wise to prepare himself for the awesome demand and absolute requirement to be honest with himself first.

The next great test for a trustworthy person is in their pursuit of true intention. Many people practice clever words and feign behavior that seem inspirational at first, but they can sometimes grow into a sophisticated form of manipulation instead.

Speaking from intimate experience, some of the kindest words and most careful instructions I have ever received did not come from those who were really interested in me. They came from the salesman, the politician, and the misguided religious people I have known and trusted.

I wish I had not been so gullible and that more friends would have protected my rather obvious vulnerabilities. All lessons are good when they can motivate us to do better and become wiser, but the harder lessons always seem to come from pain. There is nothing more valuable than an authentic friend and honesty is more than the best policy; it is the only consideration in every circumstance.

Honesty

Hole

You can never find forgiveness until you are willing to dig deeper than the hole.

Forgiveness

Honk

I hate when people reduce the world's complex problems into a bumper sticker expression. "Honk if you agree with me."

Wisdom

In Consideration

In consideration for everyone you have truly admired, notice how little they have complained.

Character

I Forget

For me, forgiving trespasses has always been easier than forgetting about them. I think it is because two different processes are at work. Forgiveness involves the heart, and because of its softness, the heart is always trying to find ways to mend relationships and move on. Whereas forgetting involves the mind, and it likes to rewind, rehearse, relive and remember every detail of the damage.

So in order to escape the pain of memory and enjoy the benefits of forgetfulness, I work hard to change my mind and use the more metaphysical qualities of my heart. I try to place my heart inside the chest of an offender, and I allow it to look for the reasons behind the transgression. Somehow when my intellect and ego are covered with a kinder emotion, dismissing an offense becomes less complicated.

The moment real compassion for our brother surpasses concern for ourselves, then forgiveness becomes much less of an effort ... but I always forget why.

Forgiveness

Indifference

Indifference is a lonely internal battle that only I can fight because no one else really seems to care.

Relationships

Irony

Many people use up their time and resources trying to get more. A much better choice is to continuously release whatever we momentarily possess. This slender thread divides those who have from those who always need more. An ironic key to having it all is proving to ourselves that we can always give it away.

Need

It's Not You

The best way to approach any experience is to not take it so personally. When someone chooses to be unkind to us, they are probably unkind to others. The same is true about people who are more supportive. As ego-driven creatures, we tend to believe everything is about us. It's not!

The only thing that really counts is how we behave and spend our gifts on others. Strangely enough, this is our most personal and important quest. Everything else that comes to us, or at us, contains enough grace for us to succeed or enough wisdom for us to duck.

Attitude

Isn't

Nothing can exist inside a vacuum or subsist within a void. Wherever goodness isn't, selfishness and arrogance are.

Awareness

Junkie

One of my biggest regrets in life is allowing myself to become a TV junkie and an air-conditioned dog. Sometimes the hardest climb we can ever undertake starts from our living room couch.

Behavior

Just

Watch out for noble thoughts and good intentions. They always show up just before nothing is done and they love to hang around just to make sure.

Action

Key

Always encourage kindness and increase its supply when others cannot. Whenever we pay attention to the goodness within people, more goodness may surface. The key that unlocks the best in others often opens the secret door to us.

Kindness

Kind Memory

When people are less than helpful, let's try to create a higher choice for them. Rather than joining the fray to push them down, aim to lift their thoughts to a better place.

Someday when we need a hand up, their kind memory of us may reach from above.

Inspiration

Library and Labyrinth

Our primary goal in life is to love and be loved, and it is best realized when we can begin to love ourselves properly and with great humility.

Life is a pool we pour ourselves into. It becomes gratifying the moment we consider it half filled by our appreciation for His gifts. As God's possession, our thoughts, words, and actions already contain His power and it is up to us to use them wisely.

The person you saw in the mirror this morning is His library and labyrinth for celestial miracles. The reason we should value ourselves more is because we are His singular precious gift to life.

Self-esteem

Loose

When a carpenter comes across a screw that can't be tightened he just moves on to the next hole to attach the bracket. This is also good advice for screwed up people as well.

Relationships

Kindness

Personal kindness can help us better than almost anything else because it encourages supporters and dissuades detractors.

Kindness

Listen

A wise man rarely speaks because his words have value. Often his silence is loud enough for everyone to hear his wisdom.

Wisdom

Magnetic

It's always good to remember that even negative people have a certain magnetic charm. It's ironic that so many of us look to them for a positive experience.

Relationships

Megaphone

Arrogance is the breath and force behind Satan's megaphone!

Attitude

Malleable

Whenever a heart becomes rigid it is surprisingly easy to break. But when it chooses to remain soft and pliable, a good heart will seal its own cracks and relearn its capacity "for-give."

Forgiveness

Mama

Empathize with those who invest so much effort to acquire money, power, respect, or prestige. They will never earn their worth or value their friends.

Nothing can purchase time, opportunity, blessings, or esteem. Pity those fooled by fashion or hypnotized by an image. In a moment, their face will crack like grandma and Oil of Olay won't help.

Let's remove our makeup before the party is over. Our warts and freckles, cracks and crevices, are beautiful and unique. After all, the coolest face that ever touched your cheek was your mama's. And the smoothest face that ever touched the world was Mama Teresa.

Authenticity

Memorable Mistakes

A selective memory of past mistakes often sets the stage for future misjudgments. It is healthy to forgive ourselves for our trespasses, but it is never wise to forget their consequences. Painful memories properly reviewed can become our most protective friend.

Awareness

Mark

The wonder of life is only in this moment processed through your thoughts and memories. Here is an idea. Actually, do something today worth remembering and make a note of it on a special calendar.

It will enhance your present, excite tomorrow, and create an inscribed legacy for the future. By this very writing, I have just marked history and created a new memory.

Mindfulness

Merry Everyday

Today on this special eve some of us may feel the warmth of memory and anticipation. However, others may feel the sadness of what was, or never was. But here is some good news and an even better gift.

As long as we are human and have the capacity to feel, we also have the power to create and change our circumstances through the adjustment of our attitude. Yes, things are difficult sometimes, but at the same time life can be glorious when we choose to notice!

This moment could be a gift card to everyone we touch that never expires. All that is necessary is our willingness to notice the good in every person and allow grace and gratitude to fill in the cracks!

We could easily share more credit, encourage more empathy, and inspire more action by simply electing to do so. We have the inventive power of love and hope at our fingertips at all times!

God's live Spirit is inside of us, so all things are possible when we allow Him to freely operate.

MERRY EVERYDAY including a joyful tomorrow!

Attitude

*(Written on the first Christmas Eve after my mama passed)

More or Less

When we care more about people who seem to care less, we actually give them more to care about.

Empathy

Move

From politicians and preachers to well healed motivational speakers, I have always heard about the good I can produce. So often my mind flows with wishes and dreams but I often fall asleep again.

This time was different! I woke up - got up, and shared this very thought with friends. It is funny how change, motion, and action seems to be behind every moving idea.

Motivation

Mystify

The selfish are the most fun to give to. You can always enjoy their surprise, amazement, and the scavenger hunt as they search for your hidden motive. Mystify a mean person today. Be kind to them!

Kindness

NRA

Once we can cheerfully absorb a direct hit from our friends, it is much easier to teach them more careful target practice.

To misquote the NRA, "It's not the frustration that kills. It's our overreaction that can destroy friendships."

Relationships

Narcissist

Like a shark to an unsuspecting swimmer, a narcissist must be discovered and avoided to ensure a healthy relationship. Unlike most circumstances where people are helped by attention, in a narcissistic relationship both parties are further damaged.

There is a simple way to discover if a person is ego driven and non-empathetic. All you have to do is ask them. They will enjoy the question; enjoy their answer, and enjoy the time you spent with them.

At your very first opportunity, slowly back away from further contact with a smiling narcissist and RUN!

Relationships

Nice

Few want instruction, correction, or advice.
Some allow it once, but never more than twice.

Most know who they are and as they are,
God's grace will for them suffice.

So rarely intrude or leap to conclude,
But encouragement is always nice.

Support

Nascent

Some relationships are like a rocket's red glare; they spark, elevate, explode, dazzle, and sadly descend, only to trail nasty memories and lots of smoke.

But inside the measured remnants of any experience are the nascent powers of a much better shot. Always use a near miss to calibrate the next load so that you can expand your range and improve your aim.

Relationships

News

Now that I am in my 60's, both my friends and time seem to be passing much more quickly. Although my strength and resources are not quite as vibrant, I certainly want to feel more motivated. It is similar to a quarterback who has not completed a pass all game but in the last 2 minutes he tries to become an all-star.

I am coming to that great part of my life when I start giving advice I never really received myself. "Live your life each day as if the clock is running out." At my age, the best I can do is get up 15 minutes earlier. But the truth is, I can only do that when I fall asleep before the late news is over.

Mindfulness

Now

I first began writing some of the ideas in this book after Katrina. Much time has passed and that fact alone is a valuable lesson.

If you have a dream, begin to turn it into reality today! Everything needs time to form and most things take longer than you imagine.

Whatever your mission may be, start some aspect of it right now before you turn to the next page. (If you feel I can help you with encouragement, I am easy to find through an internet search.)

Our travels have crossed as a result of these words. My new dream is that they can help you find your way.

Service

OK Big Shot

Many are blinded by greed to always go after the biggest piece of the pie. The truth is all that we have and all that we think we have are gifts we have not earned. Humility teaches us that every breath and movement isn't ours to command. So let us dis-enthrall ourselves from the "big shot" we think we are. Rather let's take our place at the real Big Man's table with quiet gratitude. Even if we have to sit at the kids table, it's still Thanksgiving every day.

Gratitude

One

One act of unselfish love is more effective than a thousand words from an expert.

Love

Other People's Stuff

Our message of hope should always remain the same. "We are clean in God's sight and we were not created to become a receptacle for other people's garbage."

Tolerance of foolish behavior is a regular part of daily life. But we must never allow anyone the consistent power to steal our health or disturb our internal peace. Our clear message must be: "To those who wish a victorious life, we will gladly provide support. But to those who really want less, we must sadly demand that you go away from us so that we may grow away from you."

People with volatile moods and multiple personalities can be entertaining for a time, but it is always a good idea to steer clear of people who want to pull you down as they enjoy their own chaos.

Relationships

Over Our Glasses

Opportunity is a curious thing. Sometimes it is given away and sometimes we have to take it, but it's available whenever we want to do better. Over our glasses or at the end of our nose, the next chance is always looking back at us.

Opportunity

Paralysis of Analysis

To all those meticulous people who think, read, analyze, research, judge, study, consider and reconsider everything:

PLEASE STOP!

"Rest, relax, enjoy, and chill,
Be quiet, alone, content, and still."

Stillness is God's firmest command.

Remember that you can't make a base hit if you swing too hard and you will drop a fly ball when you forget to look it into your glove.

To everyone who suffers from a "paralysis of analysis" this old joke comes to mind:

A guy walks into the doctor's office raising his right hand. He says to the doctor: "Doctor, doctor it hurts when I do that."
The doctor says, "Then don't do that!"

Sometimes the best action is less action and the best proof of our faith is found as we gently surrender. The kindest blessing to offer anyone is internal peace, and the greatest hope we can have is that it may be returned to us.

Peace

87

Penny

When you are tempted to offer your two cents into a discussion, reach deeper for some common sense instead. It is a much greater contribution because it is so rarely utilized.

Common Sense

Popcorn

We throw around the word "love" like popcorn in a dark movie theater. We don't seem to care who it hits and we especially don't care who it misses. But what if love really is the only good food that can feed our spirit and nourish the people around us? What if it is the deepest reason we rise in the morning, try to learn what we try to learn, and work at what we work at? Would we then crush it like kernels under our feet as we walk through the dim showing of our life? The fact is that many of us get caught up in viewing our life as a fantasy adventure, but in truth it is our feature love story to the world.

Without love, we have nothing. But when we pay closer attention to the person sitting next to us, we can develop a deeper empathy. Health, youth, and mental capacity will not always remain with us, but the warmth of authentic friendships will.

We must make sure good souls can always touch us, see us, and speak to us. But we must also realize that we are all children of our own experience. So we must use our precious time to share all that we have learned from others, scene by scene.

Can't you smell the fresh popcorn? Let's rise up and explode with enthusiasm so that we can all love butter... I mean better!

Love

Positive

Value the source of your light and protect it from overload or outage. When you feel more energized, it is easier to find a positive solution to a difficult circumstance.

Relationships

Paint

Some people paint pictures; others paint houses. It all depends on their need for air conditioning.

Viewpoint

Preservation

Acceptance preserves energy that suffering tries to steal and forgiveness heals much sooner than time.

Forgiveness

Progress

Thanks to the anonymous internet, behavior is now recorded and celebrated by all ages to be seen for all time. Finally, history and perpetuity have joined forces to show future generations just how little we have grown as a society.

Almost always, progressive ideas and inventions can benefit from a careful and thoughtful step back.

Maturity

Pulling a Knife

When correcting another person the experience is exactly like pulling a knife on them. The only thing they really want is a quick escape without getting cut. Because successful correction always requires the participation of the person being corrected, it should be done with grace, humor, and empathy so that no one gets further scarred or marked. If you may disagree, I am prepared for your correction.

Relationships

Pull

When you are in a difficult spot and you really need to pull off a miracle, never push good people away. You may need them to pull together so you can pull through.

Relationships

Push

Many tasks are necessary but not very enjoyable. But whenever we are able to push ourselves towards their accomplishment they can become much less difficult over time. Faith, sacrifice, and discipline are some of our highest aspirations because they can produce the greatest rewards. I know for sure that when I don't push myself, my wheelchair instantly becomes just another piece of ugly furniture!

Motivation

Perilous Journey

Maturity is the perilous journey from wise guy to wise man.

Maturity

Quiet Attention

Be careful around a ready showman. A good act can reduce our keener insights and lead to a mistaken perception. It's always better to trust a humble person that doesn't want to be noticed than a slick salesman that demands a big audience. Whenever someone feels a need to patronize us, their purpose may be to create a false impression and a true dependence. Kindness always operates better in quiet and it never requires outside attention.

Authenticity

Reaction

One of the first principles I remember learning in physics class was: "For every action there is an opposite and equal reaction."

In the area of human relationships, this doctrine works in positive situations as well, but it can be equally hurtful when people wish to use our reactions as a means to harm us.

But there is a spiritual convention of proportionate measure that is also available. "Do unto others as you would have them do to you."

God's masterstroke of gamesmanship reminds us to always serve love in response to hate. In this way, the balance remains constant, both on earth and as it is in heaven.

Relationships

91

Refresh

I have discovered it is best not to miss an opportunity to renew and refresh myself. I just figure that if it works for subscriptions and computer signals, it might also benefit me. Think about it. Isn't recess the most popular event in school and a coffee break the best use of time at work?

When was the last time you had a mindful moment alone without your iPhone, kids, dog, boss, or spouse? Can you remember the last time a hot shower was a holy and glorious experience?

These are gifts we must receive if we want to remain effective. Jesus was always surrounded by at least a dozen guys. But even He planned for private walks, a little wine, and a quiet talk with His Daddy now and again.

Mindfulness

Regular

A genius is just a regular guy who has learned to maintain control over his own personal stupidity.

Awareness

Release

The best way to keep a friend is to release him from your desire for continuous agreement.

Friendship

Resilient

We should never allow criticism to crush our spirit or ruin our day. When we remain open, supportive, and resilient, we can even view a harsh critic as a kind friend.

We know we have become a grown up the moment we can turn everything that comes our way into a beneficial experience.

Maturity

Retain and Maintain

True humility is the art of retaining the pugnacity of one's doubts while still maintaining the courage of one's convictions. Both are necessary to becoming fully human.

Humility

Rev Up

It's always fun to shift our thinking forward when we feel pulled in all directions. Nagging problems can never keep up with positive motion powered by our determined spirit.

Optimism

Rock and Roll

Be grateful for your busy day and something important to do. Many people I know sit at home in chairs that rock or chairs that roll and they wish they could take your place.

Gratitude

Rocky

As I work, I find it is better to have music inside my head rather than the noise of self-criticism. I know it sounds crazy, but when I allow my imagination to drift forward, inspirational themes seem to stream to the rescue.

For me, Rocky Balboa was never a fictional character. He was my trusted gym partner whenever I needed to climb the stairs.

Inspiration

Ruts

The ruts that are cut when we roll backward are just the curbs we need to form a better path.

Attitude

Safe

As a disabled person before the modern age of enlightenment, I was always taught to play it safe. I learned to properly fall before I could really walk, and I was forced to walk rather than encouraged to do so. Surrounded by other sidelined kids, I became a scorekeeper and an observer rather than an active participant. I was 40 years old before I could fit my wheelchair into most public restrooms and I still can't visit most French Quarter shops because of the narrow aisles.

Handicapped seating was either the best or the worst and people were either very nice to me or they treated me as if I were spastic and retarded. (Those were common adjectives used in my younger days.)

It is not true that we don't want you to help us, but it is true that all disabled people know one another. (We are a secret society that builds ramps and paints parking lots.)

Empathy

Sailing

In a healthy discussion, why are so many wedge viewpoints necessary? Is this the new popular system we now call the American way? Who decided that contention was so preferable over cooperation? Must our paradigm so often remain "we vs. them" when we seek solutions?

Here is a new twist on an old biblical idea. Let's search for a person's heart when his approach is different from our own. Perhaps we could grow to understand that some people who currently don't share our experience may also be our friend.

The voyage becomes easier once we accept that living is filled with good and bad, right and wrong, and all the areas in between. God's blue lifeboat called earth is shared by all of us. Must we always try to rock it or sink it? Can't we just work together and try to sail it?

Cooperation

Salesmanship

Whenever strong persuasion is needed to sell any idea, there is something inherently wrong with it. Every good concept sells itself to those who are best informed.

Manipulation

Show Up

Once you have become committed to seeking goodness, it's easy to find. You have just created it by simply showing up.

Goodness

Scraps

With all the new technology designed to help us, we seem to be even more harried, hurried, and hungry than ever before. Rather than understanding that life is a banquet to be savored, enjoyed, and shared we consume it alone; standing over the sink. The crumbs we spill are for the dogs and we expect our friends to fight for the scraps of our time.

But the real truth is that time does not belong to us anyway. It is God's eternal gift so that we may use it in service to His glory.

So let's calm down and sit down and offer each other good food for thought instead. The moment we stop feeding our need for self-importance, satisfaction will become an honored guest.

Generosity

Search

Compassion encourages us to search through pain until we find forgiveness. Then forgiveness multiplies and fortifies our compassion to make the next search even easier.

Compassion

Season

Just like grandma's old cast iron pot, a pale hard watermelon, or a Mardi Gras king cake in July; nothing is worse than the right idea in the wrong season!

Time

See You Later

"See you later." is a clever and heartfelt expression, but nothing in life is guaranteed. At least once in every lifetime, when those words are spoken, the expression won't tell the truth. For all of us, our earthly end is sooner than we want and it is always later than we think.

Time

Sandblast

When I was young I was rather square. I wasn't easily moved because I was more stubborn and rough around the edges. But because of the dynamism in life and the sandblasting of circumstances, I had to smooth my approach and reform my character.

If I were to advise any young person today, I would simply say that every experience is a refinement meant to increase your value, so there is no reason to resist or fear any rugged challenge.

Growth

Sale

The things we need are simpler and easier to find than the things we want. That is why monasteries have such lousy garage sales.

Neediness

Seed

*In such a discordant world, we seem to fear tolerance and inclusion
just like every generation before us. I think it's because fear hasn't
changed much over many centuries. All people, everywhere still want
to keep what they have and get more of what they want, and walls
and wire can't contain their flow from any side.*

*Here is a silly little lesson I learned as a kid. When the gravy didn't
want to stay atop my volcano of mashed potatoes, I eventually
allowed it to flow over my peas. Although I didn't like it at first, I
decided to have faith in the stronger forces of gravity and
philosophically deal with any distasteful circumstances as fact.*

*To a world in doubt, there is comfort in calm. Our inner sanctum
will always remain secure and no one can ever disrupt our ethereal
protection as long as we possess a grain of faith.*

*The deepest truth is that we can never change any part of a wider
surface until we nurture courage within ourselves. Many may think
it's a tired old expression, but personal faith is as simple as belief in a
rugged cross, a shining light, and a living seed.*

Faith

Shift

*As we enter the race again today and merge with traffic, we need only
make a shift in our thinking to prove we can compete. The boost
comes when we realize nothing happens TO us that is not exactly
balanced by everything that happens FOR us. We need only to keep
our eyes on the road and notice how we stop, start, turn and shift.*

Guidance

Shaft

"We all see through the cup darkly," as scripture reminds us. But we can only become a wide-eyed traveler once we have the courage to look beyond the dim light bulbs of our mind and train ourselves through to the other side of a difficult passage. The truth is that faith and justice are blind just so that they can help us feel our way.

We have finally grown up when we realize that life has never been about the light at the end of the tunnel. The underpass and station have always been air conditioned and eternally lit and movement through to the darkened subway invariably proves to be the most interesting part of the trip.

Attitude

Shut Up

Here is a novel idea. Let's express less and enjoy peace and quiet more. It worked well for Buster Keaton and Marcel Marceau, and Ben Franklin used it as his defense before the British Parliament.

The rain drops have a song to sing and your inner voice is always trying to share some guidance.

Listen up! That whisper you hear may be God speaking to you in His loudest voice....... stillness.

Silence

Solutions

A true friend is easy to spot. They offer novel solutions rather than harsh criticisms.

Relationships

Sincerity vs. Aggression

Whenever someone is frustrated, listen closely to their sincerity. Kind attention will defuse most misunderstandings. We are all imperfect, needy creatures that want to be heard. Words alone are worthless, but words followed by gentleness can save a friendship.

Communication

Slate

Most things are not as important as you think they are. Remember your first serious romance or your first day on a new job? Notice how time has tempered your thoughts and soothed your memory.

Good or bad, the sharper colors in life fade and history is rather kind so that we may always have the courage to draw a better picture every time we try.

Moving Forward

Smile

This is the only thing you need to know if someone is your friend. Does thought of them bring a smile to your life? Do you wish to see them, be with them, talk to them, or e-mail them?

Reaching towards someone in person or through cyberspace expresses our greatest hopes and desires. Always reach! Humans showing humanity is us at our best. Noble thoughts create prayers that encourage and ideas that inspire. So think about your best friend right now and thank him for the smile that just came to your face.

Friendship

Soar - Sore

Some "friends" are more work than owning a baby chimp! They push and try us like fitness instructors and use our goodness as their monkey bars. So choose and lose your friends carefully. Good friends help us soar to a higher place. Bad friends just make us sore.

Friendship

Soft Focus

Whenever our viewpoint encourages us to see someone in an unkind light, perhaps it is a good idea to shift position. We can never change anyone, but when we choose to see someone in a better light, the same soft focus may also reflect on us.

Viewpoint

Sort

Give only to souls who want your gifts
And cry for the ones that don't

Speak only to those who make it easy
And silent prayers to those who won't

Our life is His, and not ours or theirs
And the time He gives is short

Filter through only healthy friends
All others learn how to sort.

Choice

Sound System

The other day I was rolling through the mall. For no apparent reason, I happened to be thinking about who really had more influence in the world today, Donald Trump or Mother Teresa.

Just then, "Money, Money, Money" the theme song from Trump's old show "The Apprentice" began to play on the sound system.

Influence

Speak Up

Until God spoke the word, everything was nothing. So when you have something really important to say, do more than just keep it in mind. Speak up!

Communication

Substance

The world really doesn't care very much about who you are and it cares even less about the person you think you are. Your substance as a living organism and your value to humanity is best determined through dynamic and personal action.

Here is an idea that will radically change your life and improve your effectiveness. Every time you voice a prayer attach to it a direct and specific activity. This simple practice will fill your tool box, increase your skills, and ignite your spirit. Every substantial outcome needs both faith and dynamic movement.

Behavior

Speed Dial

With instant access to everyone through a cell phone, Facebook, and e-mail, have you noticed how poorly we actually communicate with each other today?

This thought that was contained inside my mind just a few slim seconds ago, can now lives on in your mind via your in-box or a Facebook post. I can transport my thoughts and they can arrive with even more clarity and coherence than when I first imagined them thanks to grammar and spell check. Science fiction has actually become science fact today.

But what is the value of any idea that does not move us towards action? You are thinking about someone you love RIGHT NOW. One touch on your screen and science can bring their breath into your ear. Guilt has never been a good motivator, so it is the brighter gift of awareness I am suggesting.

There is no application that can bring our lost family members back to us. As a tribute to them, please consider this thought and speed dial someone you love.

Communication

Spell

The best advice I ever get comes from my magical cat. She always aggressively tells me exactly what she needs and I swear she is speaking proper English!

It is unfair to expect even your closest friends to anticipate your wishes all the time because quite often their own wand is low on batteries. If you need compassion, it is best to show it first, and it's always helpful to have a variety of caring people to call on. There is really no trick to it at all. If you really want something, ask, and if no one hears you by the second or third time it's OK to spell it out.

Need

Spent

It's easy to create an unnecessary expense but when we work to pay it off we often become less available to the people we love. In our struggle to keep afloat, our spirit can sometimes feel the burden.

When we look at the things we have, let's also remember the good relationships we no longer possess because we were too tired or busy to enjoy them. We must realize that human greed is always boundless in the face of unreasonable desire and finite resources.

The next time you pay a bill; why not also pay closer attention? The kind investment of time with an old friend will always outshine the sparkle of anything new. Your greatest love is time well spent together. So why don't you just keep your money and pay someone a carefree visit instead?

Greed

Steroid

Some people don't know the grief they cause simply because they lack the maturity to take responsibility for it. The best way to deal with this type of pain is to simply choose not to suffer from it. Forgiveness is an amazing drug. It can be an anesthetic for us and a growth hormone for them.

Maturity

Stones

Rocks fly from us and at us all day as a result of our judgments yet a better solution is always just a stone's throw away. Let's relax our grip and our gripes and shower mercy instead. Most often the battles we fight are the battles that we have caused.

Judgment

Super Hero

In the world with so many typists and talkers, commentators and critics, it is sometimes difficult for an old school optimist like me to gain traction. I never was a fresh-faced seer who walked in sandals from his air-conditioned class to a waiting Lexus. I was a fat kid who talked some but never typed. I had one pair of corrective shoes until I was 30 and I needed to push myself wherever I wanted to go. It took me a long time to gain a higher insight about life because I was always too busy sightseeing for everyone else.

But I finally began to notice a difference between the "normal" people and me. I always seemed happier than most and now I know why. Everybody could see my handicap and braces so most people were kind to me ever since I was a little guy. I never was teased or bullied as a kid and the only people who really gave me a hard time were my physical therapists.

Somehow I got into my head that my disability was a gift or superpower to cheer people up. I learned to gain positive attention through my jokes so that when I fell into the classroom I would not be too embarrassed.

I truly believe to this day that my attitude and sense of humor are my sword and shield of protection.

Everyone has a handicap of some kind. We can all possess the spirit, mind power and personal philosophy to help overcome anything. It is just a matter of choice.

Attitude

Supersede

The best time to rise is when you feel like you cannot and then you do so anyway. Something supernatural always happens when your choices supersede your natural desires.

Transcendence

Sure Sign

Every word we speak, write, or sing either backs us up or turns us in.

Bravado is unnecessary when our words are clear. So when our temptation to speak is the greatest, just for fun, take a moment to listen instead. It's a sure sign of a rare and measured approach. Nothing is better than a well timed remark spoken with precision.

Authenticity

Take and Hold

Only people who actually take responsibility have the courage and stature to hold others accountable.

Responsibility

Talk

The information superhighway is so clogged with debris that true human connection is becoming much more difficult to accomplish. It might help if you think of talking to a friend as a new app. called: "verbal texting."

Communication

Tender

I learned a great deal about communication and relationships from my high school debate club. The star of our team was a kid we called "The Bone" because he would strip an opponent down and never let anything go. He not only would beat a dead horse; he would try to freeze it, thaw it, and tenderize it again the next day!

40 years later, I still remember his name. It was on the news tonight because he was killed in a bar fight two blocks from his family.

Communication

Tether

In any situation, we can always choose a better temperament. We will know that we have found it when we realize that we now control the tethers that others used to try to pull us down.

Attitude

Thought

Negative thoughts add to our discouragement and disillusionment. So where is the good reason in ever having them?

Optimism

To Do Then Become

When you really think about it, "to love" is much more necessary than "to be loved." The action of love makes it possible for two more people to actually "become loved". Therefore whenever you feel disconnected or unloved, all you have to do is get busy loving someone so that you may become more loved in return.

Love

Toll

When I was younger all I wanted was to be heard because I was surrounded by big voices and even larger personalities. One of my favorite biblical quotes has always been "If they have ears, let them hear!" I guess even Jesus had friends and family who were deafened by ignorance and defined by stubbornness.

I don't speak as loudly or as often anymore because I have come to realize plugged ears are less of a problem. The massive clog remains inside the beats of our rather cold and selfish heart. And over a lifetime it can really take a toll.

Communication

Too

When we are fortunate to know people that believe in our words, it is important not to talk too much or too often!

Wisdom

Treatment

Immediately resist whenever someone tries to rub you the wrong way. Your healthy body, mind, and spirit should never be pushed into replacing hard-won, hands-on experience.

Experience

Trust

Both a good liar and a truth-teller enjoy the same stature and standing for a time. But as the winds shift and the tide turns, slight changes in character soon appear. A liar usually becomes smaller and weaker as cracks surface in his foundation. And as he twists towards the prevailing winds, he often buckles under the pressure.

On the other hand, an honest person stands firm in his convictions and may grow taller as challenges come. Some even become more secure as they move beyond their scrupulous values into a deeper study and more careful understanding.

Actions, demeanor, and performance; are all attributes of a genuine friend. They are difficult to find but worthy of our lifelong search.

Authenticity

True Optimism

A true optimist has everything he needs no matter what happens.

Optimism

Two Sense

It makes sense to be an optimist in recognition of all that we possess, but it makes even better sense to be optimistic when we think we have little. I am positive this is exactly why optimism was invented.

Optimism

Tears

Tears are essential because they cut the path and define our journey. Every deep truth I have learned in my life is the result of some pain, but there is a certain facility in trying to minimize the suffering. Somehow I think it has something to do with the mystery of evil and the awesome benefits of growth.

In times of misery, I was always taught to use pain as a worthy sacrifice to a higher cause. In a small way, this encouragement really helped me because it re-framed any unpleasant experience as a noble challenge and sometimes fun experiment.

I am not suggesting that we seek out painful experiences like a biblical saint, but I do think it's necessary to be prepared for darkness by throwing a hurricane party when it arrives.

It's an old Katrina thing and the spiritual behavior of New Orleans.

Attitude

Up Front

When you live a life driven by values, motivation can be fun. The standards themselves can propel you forward, provide direction and tell you exactly how far you can go.

If you become lost, just look for a man with integrity. He is easy to find because he is the tallest man in the crowd. He is in or near the light and he always walks on the highest ground available.

Integrity

Ugh What

Wisdom not remembered is.........."Ugh What?"..........

Wisdom

Umbrella

People who can dance in the rain are not really crazy. They just see blessings inside of every storm. Great news! It's a cold and dreary forecast today. Let's put on our tap shoes and give the world our raincoat, hat, and upside down umbrella!

Attitude

USA

How is it possible that we can be such a divided and dysfunctional country when both "US" and "I CAN" are actually in the title?

Optimism

U Turn

For fun; whenever a friend tries to create a negative vibe, move their thoughts in an opposite direction. Sometimes as you turn; they turn.

Attitude

111

Viewpoint

I don't always share your viewpoint because... I don't always share your perspective. I don't always share your outlook. I don't always share your focus. I don't always share your insight. I don't always share your blind spots. And I will never share your experience!

A full life involves many points of observation. We must carefully select from those who seek us, but we should never allow anyone to sleep inside our tent without a candle. Visionary companions are rare and some lose their direction because of their familiarity with us or our complacency with them. Anyone can become easily misled by a powerful personality or a persuasive rabbi. In spite of strong influence, we must remain solely responsible for our own direction. Sometimes the Spirit requires a turn towards a friend and sometimes He requires a sharper turn away. But we must never look down upon anyone because none of us are truly lost until we call off our personal search for truth.

We must share our light in the hope of mutual clarity, but the glare will always reveal many flaws. Chief among them is our desire to squeeze from flesh and blood the higher attributes that can only come from God. Sometimes He illuminates His kids early and uses them as ornaments to electrify our path but often the shadows remain and they require a more cautious approach.

Direction

Volley

Consider your feelings if someone was important to you but you were not so important to them.

How often do we allow our partners to play tennis alone in the dark? They wait with anticipation that our service will sail back towards them with an exciting spin; only to realize that the game was never a tennis match at all but just another lonely game of solitaire.

Love must always be reciprocated. Otherwise, there is never a point.

Cooperation

Very

Sometimes the very people who we believed were sent to help us were, in fact, the very obstacles we were always meant to overcome.

Transcendence

Visionary Match

A visionary person parts the veil on how things seem and then he has the courage to walk through to view things as they really are.

Look around. How many visionaries do you see in your life? Now ask yourself if your life matches your act?

It is the most important question you will ever have to answer and it is the first thing God will ask you about.

Authenticity

You Know

A thoughtless person has no idea that he does not know.

Wisdom

3

FINAL STRETCH

Audubon Park

Seek playmates like Sawyer and Finn and not like Jekyll and Hyde. Tell hypocrisy and inconsistency to get off your see-saw*. Gently but firmly show Mr. Hyde the fence and make sure he goes. But offer a prayer to his backside because even he has feelings, a chance at redemption, and a mama who loves him.

Then fly on horses,** slide on the Shoot-da-chute,*** and climb on the monkey bars with a strong buddy who will always catch you when you fall. Or at least run home fast to tell your mama when you bump your head. Offer your friendship to everyone but save it especially for your brother who will always help you up Monkey Hill**** and never push you down.

Smell the crawfish, eat the watermelon, and watch the ball game from the top. And never allow anyone to steal the small joys of peace from your play. When you can't find anyone to climb with you; still climb...Alone.....By yourself. You are still with your best friend.

Friendship

(Colloquial to New Orleans *teeter totter **a carousel ***a slide **** dirt pile that every kid in New Orleans has climbed for generations)

Access

Almost daily I hear about a favorite author, entertainer, scientist, or political leader from my generation who has died. Sadly, most younger people only learn about them through a Google search.

With today's cult of celebrity, fame seems to be much less associated with talent or accomplishment. Sure we had our Zsa Zsa's, but they did not control all of the media in such an aggressive way. I am glad I grew up in an era when fewer people had access to everything, and connection to a wider audience was a hard earned reward for some kind of genius.

Now that most of us have a greater following on Twitter and Instagram than Jesus began with, let's use our doorway to the world more carefully than the kids do today. Because we still have a native wisdom and experience that younger people don't possess, let's employ it in a more judicious and mature manner.

In this time when everyone is paying attention and no one is paying attention, we could become a Walter Cronkite for this millennium. (For those who don't remember who he was, Google him!)

Communication

Accountable

It's always admirable to try to take on the challenges of someone in need, but we must never create a new disability for them. A successful instructor helps to grow the next generation of responsible teachers rather than support more needy students.

Responsibility

Act

If you cannot act to help your brother, then perhaps, you hide an even greater need.

Action

Adjust

Today everything seems so regimented and scheduled. How seditious would life become if we could shift the balance of our time just a little from us to them? Poverty, loneliness, crime, pollution, illness, apathy, and want would all instantly become less in every area of society. We have all heard the old expression, "There is never change without change." We all say that we want to have a better world and the best life possible. Might it begin to happen with a slight adjustment to our appointment book?

Service

All

When we can rise above the things we want, we realize that we want for nothing at all.

Transcendence

Attention

Always notice the best in people because it helps prevent their worst from seeking an audience.

Behavior

Better

Contained deep inside of anything difficult there is always an amazing opportunity to transcend it. Powered by human choice and celestial grace our viewpoint can search to meet every situation with hope. This is not "pie in the sky" but an actual reality for those who are able to receive.

The moment the spirit of loss realizes we can and must turn everything towards gain; loss itself no longer exists. In the same way light must redefine darkness, so too can our acceptance of the highest attitude recreate every circumstance.

When correct purpose greets experience, only growth is possible. Opportunity is His to give, but willing choice always remains with us. Just as worries and sadness are maintained by preference, so too is our countenance. What then is the better choice?

Attitude

Boots

Sometimes we feel a lack of appreciation because no one seems to notice our contributions. But once we realize that service is its own reward it becomes easier to graciously accept any job we are given.

Does history remember the name of the kid who caught the first 7 fish Jesus increased before the multitude? Who was the humble lady that washed Mother Teresa's habit every day? And who was the guy that always checked Billy Graham's notes and straightened his tie?

For every inspirational concert, some anonymous fan has to lug the equipment and adjust the sound system. Who will really appreciate him? We just did! The same is true with every secret effort.

The next time you see Santa Claus, even out of season, help him on with his boots. He is a little round fellow who eats too many cookies so I know he will appreciate your help.

Service

Burlesque

The problem with some who wish to become our leaders today is that they don't seem to have strong control over themselves. Few people can receive good ideas unless they come from a reliable source, and many view a person's over-reliance on money and personality as burlesque political entertainment.

If I were younger, here is the advice I wish I would have both given and received: "Early and at every opportunity conduct yourself well."

Good leadership in every field is a gift granted by others to those who can best manage themselves.

Leadership

Burp

It is impossible to remain emotionally healthy and harbor resentments of any kind. Anger and frustration are easier to manage when we are careful to hear them but unwilling to hold on to them.

Whenever anyone needs to vent on us, let's think of it as a giant burp and pretend not to notice as we smile and blame it on the dog.

Attitude

Capability

A sure way to end a depressive mood is to try something you have never done before. Even if you fail, you have proven to yourself that you have the capability to try. It's difficult to stay a pessimist once you realize that you possess the exact same qualities of an undersea explorer or a scientific genius.

Motivation

Cat

Pet people with kind words just like your old cat. Otherwise, you may get scratched.

Behavior

Catch

Life has a catch with deadlines, finish lines, and goal lines.

Practical, healthy goals do not begin as secret nebulous dreams or unfulfilled wishes. They start with a clever focus and as reachable, sacred thoughts. To those who think we are naive, we should accept their refinements with grace while still holding firm to our confidence. Mature ideas, properly vetted, form more quickly because our mind has already imagined them as helpful, visible, and viable.

After a thoughtful assessment, the next step is to awaken those qualities of faith, hope, and tenacity necessary for success. These virtues can be developed more easily simply through regular exercise. Just like a sprinter, the more we practice, the stronger our abilities will become as we push forward from fantasy to better function.

Sadly many of us remain spiritually lazy and never learn the better applications of our character. Wondrous dreams can easily degrade into nothing more than historical muses and ponderous wishes. It's partly because today we are all too busy and preoccupied with our poor habits and a need for heroic entertainment. Instead of honoring our dreams with more space, we have chosen to eat our time with lesser pursuits and silly distractions like Facebook and Twitter.

Let's all get up, take our mark, and run the race. When we fail or fade, all we need to do is catch ourselves and start again. It's rather easy to do because we are the only contestant!

Guidance

Carry and Bring

We should never allow someone's anchor to become our ballast. When bearing the burden of another, we should do so with joy as we remain fixed on our own good path.

"To bear" just means to carry and bring. It never means to become someone's sole solution or to succumb to their problems. Our endurance is not ours to give and proper perseverance always makes us stronger not weaker. When sacrifice debilitates us our reasoning is flawed. We can always help someone study and learn, but we may never take their test for them or from them.

In a ditch as a wreck, alongside someone else that we could not help, is nothing more than a twisted mess for others to clean up later. All true sacrifice is noted, but no one is more lost or dangerous than a misguided martyr.

Guidance

Chip

In this You-Tube informed generation, many more people consider themselves to be a great artist. But a camera doesn't necessarily make you into a Spielberg and a can of spray paint has yet to produce a modern da Vinci. In the field of creative expression, hard work, talent, and actual humility still play an important role.

History informs us that as soon as Michelangelo finished the statue of David, he immediately knocked the chip off his shoulder because he had a nice ceiling to paint.

Humility

Cell

I grew up in a time of the party line and busy signal. It was before the answering machine and long before caller ID. Only the most prominent doctor owned a pager, and whenever we would hear it chirp our hearts would skip a beat. (Our parents would always remind us to say a little prayer for the person in need.)

If someone talked to himself on the street, he was thought of as a little odd, and the only person who had a weird device in her ear was Uhura, the communications officer on Star Trek.

When the new push button phone came in, we would punch in songs using the cheerful musical tones and sometimes we would call Australia on accident.

Then upon the invention of the answering machine, the first thing we would do when we got home is look for that blinking red light. That little light, and the number of calls we received, soon became the instant indication of our popularity and the teenage equivalent of our self-esteem.

Now that our society has become so much more advanced, is instant communication really as necessary as the media has taught us? Am I alone in my struggle to get the attention of my friends as I try to compete with their phones?

It seems to me that if we can turn our phone off during church, we can do the same when we are with another person. Isn't respect and brotherhood just another form of church?

I know I am from a different era and these are the ideas of a contrarian, but I truly feel that the more we talk and visit in person, the better our personal communication skills will become for the benefit of all of us who are just trying to connect.

Respect

Choices

The best thing we can ever do is become more fully engaged with others and less interested in what we intend to do.

I learned an important lesson from the passing of my mama. So many dear friends promised to visit her in the nursing home, but so few actually did. For many I thought it would have been as easy as picking up a loaf of bread, but somehow their good intentions alone were enough to satisfy their deeper feelings.

For all the power of words, our soul is better fed through action. We all know we can't change the hearts or minds of anyone, but we can improve ourselves incrementally through better choices.

Speaking metaphorically, it is a good idea to clean out our cage on occasion and separate the lambs from the goats and the sheep from the wolves. But more importantly than anything else, we need to try to rid ourselves from all the bull that we love so much.

Character

Click

When things don't seem to click with someone, it's best not to ratchet up the effort. Just like an old car, some people need time to warm up to a new personality. As we easily allow space, we are not only respecting them; they are also helping to perfect us.

Communication

Circle

Retribution always does greater damage to us because it never dies easily. It lingers in the air and infiltrates all of our circumstances until it finally exposes our true character.

Character

Civility

We have all had challenging times and difficult relationships. But it has never been required that someone continue to love us in order for us to sustain a certain love and respect for them. This is often a sticky problem because high drama, hurt feelings, and long histories are involved, but a sophisticated life is all about growing above our past mistakes. The truth is that as we cultivate our character, forgiveness helps dull the sharper edges of our memory so that love and gratitude can remain.

Maturity

Clarity

Albert Camus, the French philosopher, once said: "Nothing is more despicable than respect based on fear." Somehow my youth makes more sense to me now.

Relationships

Change

The most effective changes begin with our mind, our attitude, our radio station, or our underwear.

Behavior

Clinical

A clinical examination is often a better answer than an emotional response. When we can maintain a certain facility in the face of antagonism, we have already begun to reduce the tension and solve the problem. It may seem antithetical, but intelligent restraint is often of great value simply because it is so rarely used.

Behavior

Collection

Consistently extend hope to those who offer discouragement. Perhaps they will notice you are trying to disperse the disappointments that they have always enjoyed collecting.

Encouragement

Complete

There is tremendous value in doing important things in the current moment simply because abilities tend to fade and fluctuate. Patience is a virtue but so too is actually getting things done while you still have the capacity. My daddy was a really good man, but he was a dreamer and a procrastinator. He died at the age of 58 with most of his dreams still nebulous and locked inside his mind.

Look around. Drop this book and do something important, difficult and necessary for the next hour. After you enjoy a real feeling of accomplishment , then read a few more proverbs. Your talents are finally beginning to bloom!

Action

Conduct

Do we learn more about communication from those who do or from those who don't?

Do we know more about friendship from those who treat us well or from those who can't or won't?

Our kindness, beauty, gentleness, and peace all strike a wondrous measure.

But it's from the dark, empty spaces between the notes that our music becomes their treasure.

Experience

125

Confuse the Enemy

An open heart can always be maintained with the help of a gracious demeanor. Difficult people and situations will often abound, but they can't disrupt us once we decide to remain unaffected. It's fun to defuse challenging situations by laughing and joking about them rather than joining in the fray.

He that is inside of us is much greater than he that is in the world, and we all know He has a forceful sense of humor.

Smiling into the face of adversity is a powerful statement and the confusion it causes is highly entertaining.

Attitude

Convenient Fantasy

When I was young, my doctor smoked and my barber was bald. Our teachers yelled at us and many religious were less than kind and patient. We learned about sobriety over a couple of drinks and we always talked about our diets after a second piece of cake. From this upside down perspective, an important truth emerged.

"We can never give away anything that we don't already possess."

A poor friend can never teach warm friendship and a fake person cannot see his own reality. Health only comes from the healthy and wisdom only flows from the wise. Some live with this difficult truth and some choose a more convenient fantasy, but both can help determine the person we want to become.

As a guy in a wheelchair, I may be able to share some interesting experiences with you, but please make a better choice when you need a dance partner or a ballet coach.

Wisdom

126

Continuity

Human reason is a delicate process and some philosophers believe it cannot exist alongside a provocative faith. But doesn't most scientific discovery require a reasonable leap of faith to make things more interesting? In my view, faith gives spice to our perceptions and it becomes an essential element in most exploration.

Conception, reception, and imagination all need the unseen majesty of faith. Otherwise there would be little reason for us to continue.

Faith

Count

A beautiful young friend reminded me of an ancient wisdom in times of sadness. "Count your blessings!" Here is a starting point taken from my life: Ability, Air, Awareness, Beauty, Bed, Books, Cable, Cat, Clothes, Computer, Courage, Education, Experience, Faith, Family, Feeling, Freedom, Friendship, Food, God, Good Attitude, Health, Hearing, Heart, Help, Hobby, Hope, Humor, Income, Information, Intelligence, Interest, Jesus, Knowledge, Life, Light, Love, Memory, Nature, Now, Optimism, Passion, Past, Power, Purpose, Respect, Safety, Shelter, Sight, Sister, Speech, Spirit, Touch, Truth, TV, Understanding, Water, Wheelchair, Wisdom, and Writing.

(Friendship counts double; just like in the game of Scrabble.)

Gratitude

Cookie

Everybody likes to offer their advice and opinion. But never take the last cookie from an anorexic host.

Advice

Cover

The perfect cover for someone who is incredibly selfish is to appear amazingly generous.

Authenticity

Crash Test Dummy

Learning good function from dysfunction is like learning to fly from a pilot who speaks about his near misses and survived impacts. Pain is a good teacher, but it should be reserved for poor students. Learn the first time from people who know how to glide, fly, and float. Bail from all the stunt pilots and those who insist we enjoy their sharp turns and death spirals.

Our life may not be as exciting, but for certain it will be longer and more productive. Learn only from those who can, and prove it, and move away from those who think they can, and don't.

Sure you can name those first two brothers who could fly. But can you name any of the people before them who thought they knew how to fly, but failed? The world, its Universe and even gravity honors good function. These are not our rules but His.

Flight school is open. Learn to become a successful astronaut and not someone's crash test dummy.

Guidance

Creation

Positive thoughts formulate our dreams, but only daily activity can create them.

Motivation

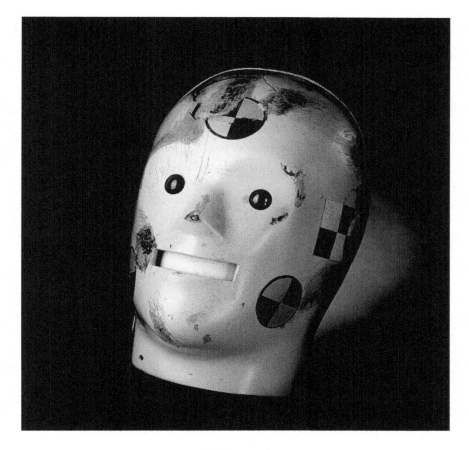

Dimwit

Riches always come to the grateful and are denied to the arrogant and selfish. Wisdom will never fit into a mind crowded and clouded by sad spirits that think they already know. To anyone who thinks this concept does not apply to them, that very thought proves otherwise.

Arrogance

Crippled

The word "crippled" was a common term used to describe my condition of Spastic Cerebral Palsy for the first thirty years of my life. "The Crippled Childrens Hospital of New Orleans" operates to this day under the moniker "Childrens Hospital". Everyone I know still refers to it as "Crippled Childrens Hospital" because disabled children benefit most from their facilities and services.

On the same street, and within walking distance for a handicapped child, was the "New Orleans Home for the Incurables". (Actual Name) It operated under that heading for more than eighty years and was known as a facility of last resort for the terminally ill. As a child, we were regularly reminded that we could be sent there if we did not behave and do our therapy properly.

At about the same time that these two organizations were flourishing, the National Association for Retarded Citizens was founded in 1950 as the National Association of Parents and Friends of Mentally Retarded Children. Initial steps for the establishment of this organization were taken in May 1950, at the annual meeting of the American Association on Mental Deficiency. The organization is now known as ARC and the word retarded has been completely removed from their name.

My point is that as a writer and a person with a crippling, disabling, handicapping, challenging, debilitating, and immobilizing condition, if you see me wheel up to a door, please offer to open it for me. I am just a guy trying to make his way and I am not a member of the euphemism guard or the vocabulary police.

Authenticity

Cure

Every time you cut someone with your tight and clever words,
or whip them with your wagging tongue, if only to be heard.

Prepare yourself for a verbal lash, or perhaps an actual stab.
Bad things do come back as a healthy scar or nasty scab.

So how can you fix these cuts and expect a reasonable cure?

First start by keeping your big mouths shut.
It's the best beginning that you can choose. I certainly know for sure.

Behavior

Dawn

Whenever you feel unloved or alone, why not use it as evidence your
focus is flawed, your vision is dim, or your eyes are partially closed?
Contrast best determines what love really is anyway. Darkness will
always better define your light, so you must allow for its division.
Enduring faith and relentless hope will always use darkness as a
counterpoint for enlightenment.

The moment you can peer through the vapor to view everything as
helpful, you will actually see the clouds lift and lighten from above.
Doom hates it when you begin to view trouble as something
interesting as you allow creative solutions to dawn once again.

Light is available in every circumstance, but you must want to find
and face its warmth. It's God's amazing personal gift to you. But
you should also remember that your reflection is your gift back to
God. After all, you were created as a mirror image.

Attitude

Draft

Observational writing is an interesting and a rather easy process for me, but I have noticed something unusual about my style. The first draft of almost anything I write sounds a little bit like a suicide note. But, as I revise and revise, the coolest thing always seems to happen. By the last sentence, hope invariably springs forth from inside of me and I think about how I can best share it the next day.

I have grown to realize that every day, every single day, I am the sole author of a new story. It is up to me to not accept the first draft, but rather to revise, revise, revise.

Attitude

Dragons

In the dark places of mood or memory, negative thoughts love to be entertained. But with the slightest change in approach or movement they will likely disappear. We are eternally in charge of our personality and character and nothing can prevent their help. On those days when I feel like I cannot possibly slay the dragon, I just get up and feed the cat. Dragons hate my beautiful cat!

Attitude

Empathize

Empathize with those who invest long hours in pursuit of money, power, respect, and prestige. They will know less about their kids, their spouse, their friends and themselves. Nothing can purchase time, opportunity, blessings, or self-worth. Let us remove all the delusions from our life so that we may see the wealth right in front of us. It's always made of flesh, blood, spirit and bone.

Awareness

Everest

With so many different ingredients in the mixing bowl of my life, I am surprised my attitude turned out so well. I always felt more criticized than encouraged, and as far as my disability was concerned my training was rigid, painful and contrived. My experiences as a kid were far different than the stories I have seen on TV about the inspirational handicapped athletes who regularly climbed mountains.

The first anomaly I can report is that I never really felt a need to conquer, prevail, or overcome anything. I was taught by doctors, teachers, and especially unsophisticated therapists to do my exercises and just accept my situation. This mindset was the norm in the '50s and it also was encouraged by my parents. I was never discouraged from doing anything physical, but I already knew my job was to be the happy observer. I was raised by Captain Kangaroo, baited my own hook at fishing camps, and cheered at all the ball games.

But here is how real disability finally took hold of me. In the interest of actually "making" a little boy walk, I was physically manipulated and emotionally maneuvered every day, from the ages of 2 to 17. When the pain and daily obligation of the Cerebral Palsy Clinic ended, I was psychologically handicapped and I remained so for years.

I thank God every day that my spirit was only damaged and not more severely broken. I suppose that without my difficulties, this rather serious book may otherwise read like a funny little pamphlet.

For every onerous memory that still crowds in from my past, I try to replace it with some positive thoughts and artistic imagery.

The next time you are faced with an obstacle that you can't possibly overcome, think of it as something less than a Mt. Everest. It might just be a papier mache' prop from your own documentary movie.

Transcendence

Expectation

Now that I am older, I have learned that human expectation is an extremely unreliable concept. It's because we expect so much from others but demand so little from ourselves.

Hope

Eleven

Carefully note all those fine people who claim their love and friendship for you. Then subtract anyone who can't or won't support their claim through personal growth and real hospitality. Finally, provide a path for forgiveness and hope that they might find their way back to the upper room again. Always be grateful for time well spent and lessons learned and never allow past disappointment to ruin a good moment with other friends.

Remember that even Jesus had to feel the pain and experience growth when He had to reset the supper table for eleven.

Growth

Edge

Our ego is fed by victory but our character is formed through defeat.

Behavior

Facebook

Sometimes when I click "friend" or "like" or I find myself typing away at the screen, I miss the funny and warm two-way conversations I used to have.

JPEGs and emails are cool, but fleshy face time and goofy phone calls are much better. Before WiFi, it seems I was better connected to myself by my actual friends.

Communication

Feed To Succeed

Consider the stress we put on our friends when we ask them to help feed our bad habits. We probably behave this way because of a sadness created over some lost opportunity. In a weakened state, we sometimes include others in our mistakes to help justify our stupidity and remain at peace with our failure.

A much better choice would be to put our nonsense on a diet and take personal charge over our actions once again.

A beautiful, smart guy can show up at your breakfast table every morning. He is the man who chooses the Wheaties more often than the cupcakes.

Self-esteem

Fumble

Be extra careful during times of high emotion. When it overwhelms us, stupidity always gets the ball.

Self-control

Funny

A good marker for high intelligence and maturity is a sense of humor. If you get a "funny feeling" when you joke with someone, it may be the first sign to move on. Lasting relationships are cemented by laughter and they often take serious effort. Life is funny that way.

Relationships

Futurama

Every time we intersect with a person's life it must be at a specific time and place. Time does not exist without an object in space. Anyone who believes that they can remain a good friend to someone without interaction with them is full of illusion. Actors inside a friendship must benefit from its relevance or they are playing by themselves, on a stage without an audience.

The solution is obvious. The past and the future aren't! We must reach for hearts of deep experience and invite them into our act right now. Only then may we help others release their gifts as we learn to graciously receive. Next, the walk through our audience must be very slow as we redistribute the gifts we have just been given. We must only allow those who know how to receive the opportunity to catch our eye, know our heart, and feel our touch. When anyone requires us to chase them, we must allow their ego to win the race. All of us are defined by the only thing we will ever actually possess: NOW!

We must learn to live life rather than relive history in the hope for Disney World's Futurama because our NOW, is now, gone....

Mindfulness

Garris Effect

I have a young friend named Luke Garris. He has such a positive effect on people that a scientific principle known as the "Garris Effect" should be named after him. In a negative situation, he always turns it into a positive event. In a neutral situation, he gives it a positive spin. And of course, in a positive circumstance, he invariably has a big optimistic reaction.

Some people hate him for his smile, but he just scoops them up and invites them into his personal Mardi Gras parade. To me, this is great love defined and the loyalty that creates it.

Leadership

Gavel

We live in a world of harsh and swift judgment, but is it really so necessary? If we lift our brother up instead, then he may be less likely to put us down, pull us down, or let us down.

Judgment

Get It

When we were young, didn't freedom mean more to us than wisdom? For the fortunate, wisdom begins to expand as we age. Freedom without wisdom is one reason so many of us suffer and cause so much suffering for others. (A quick check of the news, You-Tube, or Facebook will certainly provide sufficient evidence.) Personal wisdom and eternal grace are among the healthy reasons so many good people survive and prosper. Nothing is more wasteful in all of creation than a soul that does not "get it" because it never chooses to "possess it." At any age everyone can benefit from this simple yet profound admonition: "Wise up!"

In her last days, my mama taught me that her nursing home could be the world, when you are wise, and the world could be a closet, when you are not. In the end and at the end, she knew her bed was a sailboat and her wheelchair was her chariot. True wisdom creates everything including freedom, peace, and even more wisdom. Our choices are both its lock and the key. We can easily wait around, waste more time, and remain exactly as we are, or we can choose more wisely and move on to a better path. It is entirely up to us!

Wisdom

Greatest Gift

Sometimes the things we want most enslave us. When we use up too much energy reaching, we fail to realize all that we already possess. Let's free our brother from his imagined urgency by calmly presenting ourselves as his gift. He might realize he has enough the moment we give him all that we have.

Gratitude

Gears

Some people of high intelligence suffer from emotional or spiritual dysfunction. If that does not do them in, they sabotage themselves through bad choices or destructive attitudes. Perhaps they feel that they have to pay a tortured price for the gifts they have received.

One of the smartest things we can ever do is maintain a healthy spirit. It's easier to accomplish once we hang out with healthy people that always support and encourage us.

Proper function will always produce more goodness. So we must develop friendships that will oil our machinery and not throw sand into our gears.

Attitude

Guilt Trip

Guilt is such a vicious child that he can disrupt any hopeful journey if allowed to do so. There is only one pacifier that can manage his insidious and needful behavior. It is a Father's forgiveness.

It is the very first thing He offers us as He secures our booster seat.

Forgiveness

Get Up

It is impossible to get ahead, along, around, away, back or over until you first get up!

Motivation

Gift of the Jackass

Here is an unusual idea: Try to love the jackass.

Shouldn't we feed the hungry, medicate the sick, and provide education to the unaware or selfish?

Love is not a cruel game of "give and take" or a weapon for reward and punishment.

Throughout the ages, we have used love to manipulate, control and execute power over each other. Humanities greatest lust is not sexual. It is our lust for power to have "Our Will Be Done". We cloak it in goodwill, good work, and good intentions, but our real goal is to do what we want so that we may get what we want. We can enjoy a more healthy balance, however, by a simple adjustment towards kindness. When we allow our love to flow freely, we become less concerned about the behavior of others. We can opt for relentless love rather than feeding our expectations, demands, or selfish need. We already possess everything that has ever been hoped for in history. We can love and we are loved!

On His path through life that finally brought Jesus to Jerusalem, He did not prove His glory on the wings of an angel. He showed His true humility by final transport on a borrowed jackass.

Love

Gifted Aroma

Always enjoy the gains when someone tries to take advantage of you. Sadly some people will try to steal, cheat, manipulate, and rummage through your good heart mostly because they can. But if you are balanced, you already know a great secret they have yet to discover. There is always opportunity and growth in the garbage others need to create. So before you escort a poor friend to the curb, always be thankful for the gift of their lasting aroma.

Appreciation

Give and Take

Never take someone from their personal responsibility. Their ability is not ours to have and their response is not ours to give away.

Responsibility

Goats and Goodness

From now until our expiration date, we can allow for more purity into our lives if we wish. As ego's control over us subsides in favor of His guidance, wisdom helps reveal every snare and every clearing.

As we travel better, more healthy drink will be offered to quench our old thirst for bitter wines and sour grapes. Soon our spirit will become restored and a new desire for separation will begin to take hold. We will become much less willing to hang around nagging old goats and their kids just because our innocence will notice their smell.

Guidance

Glove

Sometimes when we become improperly focused, our approach may become arrogant. In the same way, our goodwill can suffer when fed by conceit. It can take many forms: the expression of opinion as fact, the pride of wealth, education, ability, or position, or the stridency of our denominational faith. All these destructive spirits find easy refuge inside our pretentious soul because they love the ready support of an inflated ego.

Arrogance covers, contains, protects, and warms our insecurities like a trusty old work glove. It guards our fingers against the sensitivity of human touch, so we don't have to feel the coldness and cuts of real life. Whenever we recognize this unreal situation, we must quickly remove our glove and present a naked hand towards anyone who may still want to grasp it. We need to quickly recapture the affinity we share by finally realizing the commonality of our human experience. Only then can our humility shine to help restore the security and balance necessary for a truthful and productive life.

Humility

Good Eye

Look past a person's current viewpoint in search of their warmer heart. That is actually what they are trying to find whenever they look hard at us.

Empathy

Growth

All of us come to maturity based on the conditions we find ourselves in. Inside of love, attention, and a warm environment ripening will occur in an easier way according to the proper season. On the other hand, in a hostile climate growth may be different or less productive.

Wherever you are, fully and freely create the habitat you need. God's joy is your lush spiritual prosperity. In sand or soil, fight to push your way through the rocks and roots. In whatever location you were planted, discover the best way to sprout, stand, flourish, and produce!

Maturity

Groovy

I learned early in life that the best way to stay in the groove and continue to move forward is to make a lighter impression. However, some people with a clever hook and a big personality would try to run me over. Given few options, I would either allow them to drive me away or more frequently, I would just lock my wheels.

Always remember that when a trusted friend gives you a signal to stop or yield, never hit the gas. You may need him to toss you a rope the next time you are off the road or in a rut.

Friendship

Happier Ending

The moment we learn someone is really bad news, we should close the book and end the story. Our swift and courageous action may provide the author with his own inspiration for a happier ending.

Moving Forward

Hat

I just saw an Indiana Jones movie and noticed that under every adversity the professor never lost his hat! This metaphor reminded me that whenever we search for treasure, we should always hold on to our hat because it contains our brains.

Think about it. Once we receive God as our true protector, we can begin to realize all challenges are temporary. All too often we become upset only to learn later that our reactions were fed by small, accumulated misapprehensions. As hard as we may try, we can never truly manipulate people or their situations to perform as we might wish them to. Life is not a movie script that we can memorize, so snakes, rats, scorpions and especially fear will always sneak in. But we can mitigate most difficult situations through self-control, personal kindness, and goodwill. All of us have a similar feeling, so we must respect the discomfort of others in the hope understanding is returned to us.

Friends are precious and so are we. Let's learn to give people a break because they may be under a pressure we cannot understand. It could be a secret challenge that we have already overcome.

In our world where many things are in crisis, let's learn the art of gentleness so that we may enjoy a continuing blessing rather than an accumulated curse. When we can accept all people as they are, then we can finally end our foolish search for a personal idol. As soon as maturity begins to teach us to maintain a cooler head, the world will begin to take its hat off to us. Why? Because it knows we are in our right mind and we won't easily lose it in anyone's Temple of Doom.

Self-control

Head Trip

Often we may find ourselves at a time and place that would be different if we had a better choice. Duty, obligation, or the need for a paycheck is almost always involved, so we just watch the clock and endure for as long as we can.

Being in a wheelchair, I often have to wait on other people to get me where I need to go. Rather than become more frustrated, I simply decide to use my imagination to make the experience less difficult. Here is the trick. Assuming you are not an airline pilot or a neurosurgeon, try to find a way to make any situation more interesting and playful.

Inside your mind, there is a storehouse of innovative ideas and impressive memories. Why can't a trip to the grocery store become an adventure through Aladdin's cave? Don't you remember when you were taught that a scary rainstorm was actually the angels crying and the devil bowling? What fun!

The truth is, God has given us an amazing instinct to help us through challenging times. Let's use His glorious tools to enjoy life more as we force our Millennium Falcon through rush hour traffic. (By the way, I always drive slower when it's raining cats and dogs.)

Attitude

Health

Many of my observations concern a strategy for a healthy attitude as we make our way through the challenges in life. We all experience off days now and again and we all know the value of nutritious food, proper exercise, and enough sleep. But if optimism and productivity remain a struggle for an extended period, perhaps there is an unknown physiological cause. Diabetes, high blood pressure, and brain chemistry can all affect our proper function.

Without hesitation or guilt, always take good care of yourself! You can only share health to the degree that you already possess it.

Proper Function

Heed

Whether you give attention or pay for it, both are highly valued because if you lose it................?

Communication

Higher

As children, we are taught to reach and work for the things we want. Unsatisfied, life teaches us that the needs of our higher-self are always on the highest shelf.   Now with the benefit of reflection, is there any better reason for all of us to grow up?

Maturity

Humility

The beauty of true humility cannot be taught through humiliation.

Humility

145

Homework

What was I thinking? Writing a book, even a small one, was like signing up for endless homework! To make matters worse, I have now given a big red marker to everyone I have ever met.

But between these lines and inside these pages there is a secret message. Even an average student who works at it every day can stand up to correction and make a meaningful contribution.

In anything you do, you don't have to start off great or even good. All you have to do is begin. Add to your project a little each day and progress itself will help motivate your actions.

As for me, the first words herein came from frustration, and 35,000 words later they express my growth, gratitude, and satisfaction. Work your dream every day and allow my thoughts to partner in the effort. I can't do your homework for you, but I can check your spelling and clean the eraser.

Growth

Human Satan Saint

A life not felt isn't much! It's the real reason we do, think, and pray. How much we feel and what we feel actually creates in us a human, Satan, or a Saint.

Feelings

Hungry

It is amazing how we insist our ego be fed as we allow our kindness to be starved.

Kindness

Hunt

Let's search for the treasure in everyone we meet. For some, their goodness is obvious and easy to see, but for others it may require a careful scavenger hunt. It is always worth the challenge because whenever they cross our mind, memory, or path, the experience is both our treasure and reward.

Optimism

Individual

Just like a single drop equally adds to the ocean or a separate grain increases the vast, solitary desert; every specific unselfish act expands the significance of your love in the world. It is the sole reason you were imagined and it is the main reason you are still alive.

Love

Irritating Solution

Unless you are on a roller coaster, it is impossible to laugh and be afraid at exactly the same time. I think it has something to do with the physics of adverse forces. It is much more difficult for fear and aggravation to pull you down while laughter is lifting you up.

A good strategy to use when things are difficult and cause extreme irritation is to think of a clever wisecrack or prank instead. Anxiety will almost always exit because it can't take a joke.

Behavior

Intelligent-Unaware People

There seem to be more intelligent-unaware people currently than ever before. Shouldn't we all be more cautious because many run our governments, schools, churches, and households?

Anyone can express their viewpoint today and have it published instantly over the internet. Few have the wise edit of Walter Cronkite or the careful review of Benjamin Franklin. The radio, TV, newspapers and blogosphere must find material 24/7 365 to maintain their power to influence. Therefore, both entertainment and the audience have become more important than the quality of our news content. In this environment, many ingest falsehood more easily and seem to accept opinion as fact by giving it the voice of authority.

Instead, let us turn on our spirit-guided radar and begin to prize reason once again. Let's take back some of the responsibility we gave away to the actors and commentators that lack our common wisdom. Only then may we seek the kind of truth and justice that is free to question the American way. (I think even Superman became more reflective as he reviewed his career.)

We must find the courage to question everything and everyone including ourselves. Then we can feel free to grow in wisdom, maturity, confidence, and faith through the value of our experience.

Responsibility

Intention

Human intention is a curious concept. It often produces the beneficial feelings of high achievement without requiring a single sacrifice to realize them. Be wary of anyone whose reputation is only that of possessing good intentions. Their hack contribution to any cause may be that of disruption, promise and procrastination.

Behavior

Internal Compass

If we think of confusion as one of the more interesting aspects of life and just part of our travel plans then it becomes less debilitating for us. Our All Mighty Friend is the inventor and re-inventor of our opportunities and He is always in charge and on our side.

When our path is smooth we should have fun and not allow anything to slow our progress. And guess what? The same is true when we are faced with any challenge. The blocks and boulders are just our street signs and directional signals. Enjoy the climb, the dig, the push, the pull and the wait. Life can be this simple: "Wherever you go, there you are." Take a moment to relax and check your internal compass.

Perseverance

Intersection

Sadly, there is no stopping some people who want to remain on cruise control. Their course is set and their life is already mapped. But some of us like to go out of our way because we know that there is a discovery in every detour. Every time we take the road less traveled, our driver's education is advanced. Quite often at the intersection of unknown paths, a better direction is found.

Guidance

Is

*Truth always lies beneath appearance
Because it really hates show-biz.
It's even more powerful than Faith and Hope,
Because it always IS*

Authenticity

149

John Arthur

What happened to that smart kid I once knew, on the day he really got it? Was his faithful mama next to him when his ambition turned to health and his purpose became joy? Surrounded by all those attractive youthful personalities and the awesome pull of earth, how did he find his way to the real thing? I don't know how, but I do know why. God needed a true winner and a peaceful young man!

Character

Left Hand

Sometimes by mistake we may get involved with troubled people just for the excitement or entertainment they offer. But it is always wiser to retreat from the self-destructive and move towards people who want to be helpful and constructive. Whenever poor choices cause people to fall and collapse, it is important that their debris and rubble does not damage us as well. In every personal disaster, survival of the "regular friend" is necessary. They are always needed to collect the dead heroes, restore calm, and manage the aftermath.

In times of great difficulty, no one really wants to deal with the heroics or histrionics of a fake prince, preacher, or knight, and few can ever manage the drama of a queen.

Stable folks just want practical help from regular people who will actually help them. Talk and theatrics are always cheaper than action. So the first step toward becoming an extraordinary friend is to simply be an ordinary one. People just want someone they can trust that will help when they can, and shut up when we can't. Most problems can be mitigated by our consistent, down home buddies. And our left hand has all the fingers necessary to count them.

Friendship

Monday Morning

All that we are and everything that we do remains less until we choose to become more effective. Let's demand more from our talent so that we can sustain our drive. When we really desire a better effort we can score the goals on Monday morning that we missed from our couch on Sunday afternoon.

Effectiveness

Most Efficient

Arrogance is a most efficient sin. It lets our tongue convict us even before we know we are stupid.

Judgment

Movement

I was trying to listen to a politician on TV this morning when I realized my priorities have radically changed. I was much more interested in moving to find the remote than I was in the movement of his tongue.

Motivation

Never One Without the Other

Acrimony is the price we pay for every destructive act, but a testimony is a gift we receive when we complete the final test.

Sowing and Reaping

151

North

Reduce the breeze inside your mind that stirs the smog of worry, fear, ambition, hurt, and loneliness. Pass through the clouds within your thoughts and allow the mist to settle. Begin to notice that most spirits are not dangerous but just other souls trying to find their way through the veil. Sail into areas only you know well and travel through the sudden storms with true friends who seek your company. Choose every nationality, wisdom, knowledge, and opportunity that experience will allow. And become most graceful to the somewhat lost who think they have completely found.

Move with clarity, charity, and confidence towards the ones close by on your already charted course. Reach first for the willing that want to be touched and allow them the same clear access. But be warned of the shallows inside a man's soul. His muck and mire will always produce a nasty snag.

When our brother gets stuck in the swamps of life, we must try to reach for him up to our shoulders and rib cage until our tendons pop. But life is such that we may be grasping at nothing because our rescue is not wanted. Sometimes in our attempts to help others, we lose the grip on friends already on our lap or in our boat. A smart captain remains captain to all and protects those still within his charge. He never allows himself to be pulled overboard; lost, wrecked or food for the fishes just because another crew member has chosen to jump. Our last best hope may be the first thing we should have done: release him to his fate with kindness, grace and understanding with the full knowledge that another is his master.

As we move on, let us stand regal in our wheelhouse, wary of distraction but never frightened by the fog. May our gaze remain sharp and forward and our compass always point north!

Direction

Not Yet

A person of character is kind and open during a disagreement because he knows his education is not yet finished.

Relationships

Only Three Types

There are three types of people on earth: the selfish, the generous, and the most hurtful of all, the selfish that believe they are generous.

Authenticity

Opinion

Many intelligent people overestimate the value of their opinion. But this is just my opinion.

Opinion

Our End

Our end begins the moment we become used to the world that we have created.

Growth

Our Friend

Grace is the ability to see difficulty as a good friend who simply wants us to become better.

Growth

Oz

Who among us is real?

For emotional protection, some people learn to use a different personality for each circumstance. This can be a practical solution until trust and consistency are compromised. Smart people soon learn to be wary of multiple moods hidden behind the same eyes. Plastic personalities offer the shield and entertainment that showmanship provides, but at the cost of a confused and segmented soul. Sadly, the most well-meaning people can lose their credibility in search of wider acceptance.

When we allow a projected image to disconnect us from our authentic self, neither fully exists anymore. From the beginning of human history and still today on the news, we see the lesson of many well-produced acts uncovered.

Few people intend to become a fake. But cheap renovation is tempting whenever hard work is required and natural ability is lacking. Justification and good intention have always lied to us since the turn of Adam. Even a good man can become a sneak, a deal maker, or a "don't ask, don't tell" artist so that he may remain a star to himself and an idol to his friends.

Some find their authenticity early and they remain consistent throughout their life. These are the people we should look for, honor, and allow to become our guides. Otherwise, we can easily waste years suffering through missed opportunities before we might find reality for ourselves. The saddest and most dangerous people to know are the players who never realize that their lives have become a silent movie on a cheap Hollywood set. The fear of every man in every generation is that his life has become meaningless as he allows it to flicker away.

No matter our education, temptations, or protective justifications, we must end the divisions inside. We need not always approve, but we must accept our singular personality. We must work to become the same authentic person to all. Only after we have done so may we find sanctification through our unification. We must confront our arrogance and subdue its need to control us and manipulate others. We must turn away from anything that has a deceptive purpose and invite spiritual courage back into our life. As we conform to His image; selfishness challenged by courage becomes unselfishness; arrogance becomes harmony and anger transforms into forgiveness. But the greatest benefit of all comes when we replace our desire to control others with a willingness to control ourselves instead.

Just like the Wizard of Oz, we no longer have to pull the levers or press all the buttons. We can step from behind the curtain with confidence in our God-given gifts of intelligence, courage, and heart. We then can offer to the world the pleasure of our singular personality – indivisible; as we find our way back home again.

Authenticity

On Purpose

By graciously receiving from a friend you are actually giving them a great gift. You are helping them fulfill their purpose.

Gratitude

P C

Good progress is always preceded by better choices.

Wisdom

Peace

There is a benefit offered from on high that has been available to you since The Garden. Few have it, but all need it. It was the only thing that allowed Mother Teresa to keep smiling through the filth and it will continue to help you today as you face your own challenges . An elk needs it to drink and you must have it to get a restful sleep. It was given to you from a Prince and He will maintain its flow as you learn to increase it.

Those who have it want more and those who don't, live in need of it. It is the difference between true happiness and everything else.

It is Internal Spiritual Peace.

Pluck it from the tree of life. It's the apple engraved with your name on it. Peace is the first among your Daddy's gifts. And it is the last one you will ever need because it encapsulates His divinity.

The pasture is lush and green and the water is still so that you may drink. When you can receive peace from its source you can actually change the world through your continuous offering. Peace, turmoil, apathy or denial each carve a path. The direction you take and discretion you possess belongs only to you.

Peace

156

Pull or Shoot

Whenever someone tries to appeal to my fears, the first thing I do is remove their motivation. I quickly elevate my thoughts so that angst can't reach me, and soon, nothing can either pull or shoot me down.

Optimism

Picnic

The kindness we give to others also becomes a gift for us.

After He was finished speaking and thousands were getting their fill, don't you think Jesus found a place on the grass to enjoy a snack with His 12 buddies? Every time we share whatever we have, He is right there with us holding the basket; feeding the ants and squirrels.

Generosity

Play

Why do we hesitate to express our love today but we seem to have no qualms whatsoever about voicing our disapproval? How would we all change if we became embarrassed to hurt one another? Why can't we just think like little kids once again? Remember when we loved freely, forgave more easily, and thought everyone was, or could be, our best friend?

Think back to the joy we had as children. We were cute and kind and we look remarkably the same today. Why not just roll around, get dirty, run, laugh and play again? On our front yard, years ago, we were the good kids that taught the entire neighborhood how to love.

Love

157

Point Break

Hey relax! It's always more productive to prove your maturity than your point.

Maturity

Quickly and Quietly

In an environment of gossip, debate, criticism and wild opinion, it's easy to spot the smartest person at the office Christmas party. He is the really nice guy quickly eating the free food and quietly searching for the fire escape.

Wisdom

Refine

Demanding perfection from anyone formed from flesh, blood, bone and sinew is a ridiculous expectation. Although most people declare their desire, only a few can sustain the results of their best efforts over time. But there is something each one of us can do beginning at the end of this very thought. We can clear our minds and focus our aspirations on becoming just a little bit better every day.

We are the wellspring of every improvement, even those that come directly from God. During our next activity and for each one that follows, we can push forward a bit more. As we clean, think, write, travel, work, share or rest, opportunities for a slightly sharper performance will always present themselves. Soon the small incremental benefits of our improved behavior will encourage us towards even more joyful exploration and growth.

Of course, perfection is never gained, but refinement is never lost.

Growth

Right and Wrong

Ever notice that the man who has to be right always has a little something wrong with him?

Wisdom

Re-Gifting

Now that Christmas has just passed and so many wishes for a visit or a call still remain just a wish, please consider this thought instead.

Too much concentration on our own needs can cannibalize a healthy spirit. Perhaps it would be more honest to confess that we are somewhat relieved that our latest family endurance contest is over, at least for another year.

For me, it's not so much the personalities in my life now that make Christmas such a challenging experience. It's the memory of many friends and family that have passed on or moved away that hurts.

Maybe this is an odd strategy, but I try to remember that Christmas is just an arbitrary date set by the Gregorian calendar. I know that King Gregory did not intend to upset me, so I try to be OK with it.

If we are healthy and balanced, the spirit of Christmas should live within us always without a painful memory.

When you are feeling the holiday blues, please know that I really understand and I am actively sharing a prayer with you. Now let's drink some eggnog, toast a very special birthday, and hit the pillow a little early tonight. The half-priced sales tomorrow are awesome!

Attitude

Responsibility

Without response, ability does not matter.

Action

Shall Not Injure

When struggling with any frustration, consider the transcendence of:
"Thou shall not injure thyself anymore."

How would our circumstances actually change if we made this simple daily choice?

Would we still wear those shoes that look so good but hurt so bad? Would we ever forget our seat belt, winter coat, flu shot or mama? Would we keep our word better, our checkbook balanced, our grades up and our bills down? Would we pray more, laugh more, hug more, read more, rest more, and actually be more? If we were not our own worst enemy for just one day would we be flabby, frustrated, angry, arrogant, unaware, or stupid? Isn't it true that all of us would smoke less, eat less, gamble less, worry less, fuss less and do nothing a lot less often?

Lost loves and lost opportunities would finally find a home and a rest outside of our minds and memory. We would give ourselves a break and always have a little something extra for a buddy who needs one because he is already broke or broken.

We then could look up, lift up, stand up, and cheer up. Peace would fall on us like rain and joy would jump from us like popcorn. Whenever we seek His Divinity we would also see it in our brother and sister. Our eyes would awaken to everything God has invented because we finally made peace with the best of His creation_____ (insert your name here).

"Thou shall not injure thyself anymore" is His connection with us and our new partnership with Him. Good choices would cement us and remove from evil its most potent weapons: self-doubt, self-deception, and self-destruction.

It's time to enjoy the buddy you know better than anyone else: YOURSELF. He was formed and fabricated to be your best friend from your very first breath to your very last gasp!

Self-esteem

Said and Done

When all is said and done, notice how much more is said than done. "Do the right thing" was the first thing your mama taught you, and it is the last thing you will remember about her.

Thanks to all my friends who always do the right thing. It helps me remember my mama and now I hope you are thinking about yours.

Behavior

Soul

It's the vital force that emanates from all of us, but only a select few know how to use it to connect. It is found in deep music and spicy food and young people who think they are old. It is at the core of a timeless city or movement and it is always protected by the wisest people. It is hard to find and easy to lose, but it is the very last thing we hope to see rise from within us.

For better or worse it lives forever, and it was only created to be saved and placed into His hands.

It is our singular spirit and immortal soul!

Inspiration

Stand

Whenever you help a disabled person do so with humor, warmth, and sensitivity. If they are blessed to still be active, they must ask for help often and it can be rather tiresome.

You will realize that the old "do unto others" thing has a way of providing balance, especially as your own legs begin to give out.

Sowing and Reaping

Space

At times, the best thing we can offer a friend is distance. In our passion to provide help, we may sometimes come on too strong. On accident, we hurt feelings and damage open hearts that may need time and distance to heal. Unintended damage from a friend always hurts more and takes longer to mend than intended damage from a stranger. If we want our friends to be sensitive to us, we must first be more sensitive to them.

Try to ask for forgiveness whenever you are not gentle with your friends and notice when they need some space. Do more than just allow it; encourage it, because that is what a true friend would do.

Relationships

Spigot

Is there anything that could improve your life more than the individual choice to become less fearful and more faithful?

Why are so many people angry, frustrated, and especially apathetic today? Why do "how to", "self-help", and "religious" books seem to fly from the shelves?

Could it be that our strongest cravings stream from a need for truth and actual security?

For just a little while, let's try to stop advising other people and seek self-mastery instead. Both sinners and saints love influence. But real capacity can only come from the Source. All authentic ability is spiritual. It can only flow through our faith, and it is always clogged by fear. A life gushing with purpose is rewarded with a warm shower of optimism and joy towards others. But it can only spring forth when we have the courage to turn on our own spigot first!

Faith

Stir

Every move we make is reduced to this common choice. By our actions, we can either encourage a situation to become better or help it become worse. Whenever we feel powerless, we can exercise our creative intelligence to improve any circumstance by our more mature engagement in it. Our life can brighten, darken, aggravate or enhance every moment and the people contained inside. But when we realize that things happen and everybody makes poor choices, we can inspire growth by working on our own healthy reactions first.

Some people love to stir us up and pull our strings to get an interesting response. But in real friendships, there are no strings attached. Our most powerful stance should be one of serenity because most often it is the other guy who is more mixed up.

Self-control

Take Your Time

My mother's favorite saying was: "Take your time but hurry up!"

Just like most good expressions the meaning is both basic and helpful. In this context, "Take your time." means to use your intelligence and resources to carefully get ready for the next opportunity. It encourages us not to rush into any situation unprepared.

Although the second half of the expression "Hurry up!" seems to give the opposite advice, it really does not. It simply spurs us to act in a timely manner so that we don't miss out on a good chance.

My mama was a girls basketball coach. She would remind the team that the game was just like practice. She would tell the ladies to first clear the lane before they set their feet. Then at just the right time she would yell, "Take the shot! "

They often won in the last second by two points!

Preparation

The Difference

The differences between a big talker and a truth teller are easy to determine. A know-it-all will tell you about all the good things he or she is going to do. An honest person will just quietly do them. The creator of any thought written, sung, or spoken is really a fake until his words become flesh.

Authenticity

The End

Under pressure, we sometimes see the worst in people, but we may also see them at their best, if we really want. The internal mechanism that determines our best behavior can be as simple as our faith. Do we believe that whatever happens to us, we will still be OK, or are we wrapped by an unknown and unreasonable fear? In most cases, we can better determine good results by an intelligent and spiritual approach to any difficult situation. In the end, wouldn't we all like to be remembered for the elegance and dignity of our behavior?

Faith

Things I Lack

On this special day in late November, I wish to list a few things that I lack: poverty, illness, blindness (spiritual and otherwise), space on my hard drive, stupidity, cowardice, an empty stomach, fear, a poor attitude, loneliness, enemies, ignorance, or a handicap of any kind. But I particularly lack the patience and humility to tell all the people in my life just how important they are to me. Every person I have ever known has fulfilled me in some important way. For all the goodness I have received, my thanks are sincerely given.

Gratitude

Transcendence

What is really necessary for a successful life? It is inside the scrapes at the bottom of an empty barrel and along the sides of a mixing bowl our mama just used to make a cake batter. It is the smell of fresh coffee brewing on a Sunday morning, the reason we love a Friday, and why we always start our diet on Monday.

This essential quality closes our eyes safely at night but keeps them open all day as we work or study. It is transcendent optimism!

Pioneers want it to plan, farmers need it to plant, and sports fans must have it to root. God tells us with proper faith we can choose His optimism as our daily bread. It is the first impulse behind any good cause and the true nobility necessary for every global movement. We have been offered this gift every day so that in any circumstance we may know in advance that we have already won.

Attitude

Tommy

If you thought the deaf, dumb, and blind kid sure played a mean pinball; wait until you see him play paint-ball!

Behavior

Two - Thirds

The truth about gravity is that when someone is actively pulling you down, it is virtually impossible to lift someone else up at the same time. It's always hard to be the person in the middle because they are allowing competing forces to stretch their limits. Always choose a direction and kick the southern most contestant, so that at least two-thirds of the team can win!

Relationships.

165

Today

Many seem to quote music lyrics more than scripture now, but I never could sing or dance. So here is an old verse instead:

"The thief comes only to steal and kill and destroy; I came so that they may have life and have it abundantly." (John 10:10)

Every time we give, build, and help people live, we are dancing in countermeasure to destruction itself. Is there any better reason to get up a little early today?

Mindfulness

Truth

We have often heard that the truth hurts, but isn't continuing to live with a lie even worse? We only have one life and one chance to get it right. Perhaps pain is a grave marker of something raw and real about us that we must learn to overcome. Is discomfort really such a bad thing in the pursuit of something better? After all, the more muscular people we know tell us that there is even great gain associated with it.

The truth is we are all cowards, but we can also learn to become quite courageous when we make the right choice.

Wise Hebrew words speak about the amazing qualities of gospel certainty. They say that the truth may hurt, but it can also sharpen, perfect and comfort us as it springs us from jail. This reality teaches us that as we become more honest, we soon realize that there is no higher or more worthwhile goal.

Honesty

Unmitigated

Within the tiny spaces inside like and dislike or on the narrow cracks between love and hate a commonality exists. Humans tend to enjoy fellow creatures that agree with them.

Why not allow hope to broaden your perspective and expand your heart instead? The only thing love really needs is room, free participation, and less demand for stridency and detail.

Friendship

Us

We can verbalize and vocalize in a hundred languages and a thousand dialects but who do we know that can actually speak in fluent human?

We are mortal, anthropoid, biped, hominids and as such that is all that we will ever be. (Until later.) But when I turn on the news lately, I feel like I am walking into the bar scene from the first, third, or fourth Star Wars movie!

What is wrong with us? I don't exactly know either, but I do have a sincere suggestion.

However many ears we have, we should cock one towards the creature we are trying to communicate with. If we don't understand them, we should choose an eye and look directly at them. Whatever the shape of their eyes or whatever the number, we should notice that our image is always reflected back to us inside of their stare. We are not only similar to everyone else, we are exactly alike!

Shouted, whispered, or silent, the message of humanity is inclusion and no one should ever be allowed to feel alone or alienated.

Brotherhood

Walk

Not everything in life enjoys the same priority. Sometimes we should reduce our passions over the smaller things, to help increase our endurance and effectiveness when needed. Stated more simply: a good helper must learn to rely on his measure of faith.

Although His official ministry was just over three years, Jesus rarely hurried. He was surrounded by stubborn jackasses and He walked everywhere He went........ sometimes without the necessity of land.

Relaxation

Where Y' at

As I come to the end of this treatise about direction, attitude, faith and motion, I am also beginning to understand the true value of loving a person just as they are. When we can still love someone fully without requiring change, fidelity has begun to redefine us.

Maturity

White Chocolate Mocha

Ever wonder how many $6 Grande White Chocolate Mocha Frappuccinos Mother Teresa ordered from the Calcutta Starbucks?

Appreciation

Win-Place-Show

Who we are is first.
What we do is a close and important second.
Who we say we are, and what we say we will do, is all for show.

Authenticity

Win – Win

We can help remove the intensity of any current experience by simply shifting our attention towards anticipation for the next scheduled event. All things do work together for good for those of noble and kind purpose.

Our true goal in life should always be hope because it inspires confidence and calm in every situation. When we can view defeat as completely natural and necessary then we can actually create an invincible spirit within. A hopeful warrior is perpetual because he can find wisdom in every outcome. Temporal victory can never fool him because momentary defeat can never hold him.

Hope invariably counts every loss as a future gain as it becomes our actual nourishment and motive for the next challenge.

Hope

Wisdom

As we review our words mindfully, notice the many contradictions in thought, memory, or mood. When we expose ourselves honestly, sometimes logic is not an important part of the process. We shouldn't despair or feel overly confused. Wisdom is so smart that she often appears on both sides of the same discussion.

Judgment

Who is Right?

As we mature, empathy for some harsh critics becomes much easier. Perhaps it's because we begin to understand that some of our detractors are just former teachers who have lost a measure of their passion. Or maybe others have developed a bad attitude simply because a tragedy has diminished their hope.

(Some of my friends have even told me that they like to give me a hard time, on occasion, just because my reactions are more entertaining than a Broadway musical!)

For whatever reason people criticize us, we can always give them the respect they could not offer in return. Exposed and refreshed by our simple example they may eventually become a trusted friend and less critical the next time.

Empathy

Wishes

We are the thoughts we entertain. We can never become more when we think less of ourselves.

Self-esteem

Word

Our word is a most unique gift. Giving it is worthless but keeping it is priceless.

Integrity

Write

Memories fade and history runs, but if you really wish to be remembered, write.

My mama died shortly after Katrina, but I have the notes she wrote in the margins of the books she read. They swirl and run together, but I can still hear my mama talking. She was wise, funny and confused and a deep reflection of the person I am still becoming.

Many people who know me now wish they knew Ms. Nell. By reading my words and feeling my thoughts, they do.

Wisdom

Whenever

Whenever we meet someone new or visit with an old friend, what do we always hope for first? Is it their kindness or their opinion?

Opinion

Wrong

People who believe that they must always correct others are WRONG!

Judgment

You

Do everything with humility and modesty as if you are in the actual presence of God. You are.

Awareness

You Think?

Encourage thoughts that serve you well because it really does not make sense to harbor ideas that are counter to your good and noble purposes. When you need to move, the very last thing on your mind should be ways to slow momentum and when you need to stop you must first perceive it as a viable solution.

Become friends with your imagination and revere your thoughts. The best way to improve the person you think you are is by elevating your thoughts so they can actively change your mind.

Mindfulness

Zealot

Beware the zealot of every fashion.
Most possess intolerance and lack compassion.

Willing to die and also kill,
Disagree with some and they certainly will.

Bring kindness, intelligence and balance instead.
It's better to be alive with love than a zealot who is dead.

Intolerance

Finally

Shortly after the trauma of Katrina I set out to compile some thoughts. Thank you for reading them and I hope that you have enjoyed some benefit from them. These are but a few of the many things I have learned over the past several years. With patient help, I have grown away from some of my disabilities to become a much more able person. In addition to recalling some of the circumstances that have touched my life to lift me up, I also wanted to remember some of those situations that were filled with a less gentle touch that may have knocked me down. It is from these rougher experiences that I have learned the most.

God will always give us His invincible Spirit to overcome difficulty when we simply employ our talents and enjoy ourselves according to His purpose.

However, the best lesson I have learned from my "wheels coming off" is to relax and enjoy the sleigh ride! We can actually smooth our movements whenever we reduce our ego and minimize the influence of anything that might want to drag us down.

We were all created to succeed. So fill your life with radiant people that will brighten your path. When challenged, always move to the highest road to avoid the traffic and gridlock from those who don't know the way. Seek awareness and wisdom around every turn and never fail to share all that you have received. But most importantly always continue to move forward on wheels or bare feet towards a place of growth, peace, and authenticity.

What should you do when the wheels come off? Walk towards the people and places that will fix your flats and always push you forward!

Michael J. Giusti

ABOUT THE AUTHOR

Michael Giusti is a retired advertising executive from New Orleans.

He is a former council member for the LA. State Planning Council for Developmental Disabilities as well as a former board member for the United Cerebral Palsy Association of Greater New Orleans.

Mr. Giusti was elected to the Republican State Central Committee of Louisiana and he held that position for 16 years.

In addition to enjoying reading, writing, and political research, he is an avid poker player.

93991384R00099

Made in the USA
Middletown, DE
17 October 2018